Functional Programming in PHP

by Simon Holywell

 a php[**architect**] guide

Functional Programming in PHP

a php[architect] guide

First Edition: August 2014 (Version 1.0)
ISBN - print: **978-1-940111-05-6**
ISBN - pdf: **978-1-940111-07-0**
ISBN - epub: **978-1-940111-06-3**
ISBN - mobi: **978-1-940111-08-7**
ISBN - safari: **978-1-940111-09-4**
Produced & Printed in the United States

Disclaimer

Written by	Simon Holywell	**Editor-in-Chief**	Beth Tucker Long
		Managing Editor	Eli White
Published by	musketeers.me, LLC.	**Technical Reviewer**	Koen van Urk and
	201 Adams Ave.		Oscar Merida
	Alexandria, VA 22301		
	USA	**Copy Editor**	Beth Tucker Long
	240-348-5PHP (240-348-5747)	**Layout and Design**	Kevin Bruce
	info@phparch.com / phparch.com		

For Marion, Damien, and Ariana.

Ngiyakuthanda! Ngiyabonga ntombenhle!

Table of Contents

About the Author

Simon Holywell is the lead developer at Mosaic, Brighton (http://emosaic.co.uk) and is passionate about web application development and motorcycles. His first public project was written with PHP 3, and since then, he has worked with every version of PHP and dabbled in Python, Scala, C, JavaScript, and more. He is also the author of the ssdeep extensions for PHP's PECL, Facebook's HipHop Virtual Machine (HHVM), and MySQL.

Blog: http://simonholywell.com
Twitter: @Treffynnon - http://twitter.com/Treffynnon

Acknowledgements

Many very supportive people were involved in the production of this book, and I would like to thank them for their keen insights and guidance. They helped me to take it from an idea to a fully-fledged book.

In particular, I would like to thank Beth Tucker Long who has been instrumental in bringing you this book right from the earliest of stages.

I also appreciate those who helped me formulate ideas and reviewed early drafts - especially Craig Bendell and Jamie Matthews.

To technical reviewers Oscar Merida and Koen van Urk, layout and diagram wrangler Kevin Bruce, Eli White, and Lori Ann Pannier for their contributions.

FUNCTIONAL PROGRAMMING IN PHP

Introduction and Prerequisites

Over the course of the past twenty years or so, functional programming has seen a slow and steady growth. This has led to many languages adopting functional aspects, including the much-maligned PHP. As computer hardware improves along with language support, it is important to begin learning the basics of functional programming. Whilst it is true that programming in this style requires a change in thinking, you will find that some understanding of it has a positive impact on your object-oriented code as well.

So let us begin our journey through the functional aspects of the PHP language.

A Severely Abridged History

Functional programming has its roots in the mathematics formalized by Alonzo Church who worked on various mathematical problems, amongst one of which was lambda calculus, in the 1930s. This is a system to solve complex problems by using mathematical functions that accept functions as parameters and return other functions - but more on that later. This concept lays the groundwork for the beginnings of functional programming, but despite academic interest, there was little progress until the late 1950s.

Jon McCarthy, a professor at the Massachusetts Institute of Technology, developed an interest in Church's work, and in 1958, released the Lisp (a play on List Processing) programming language. It was to become the de facto standard in artificial intelligence programming and brought a number of new concepts to computer science itself.

Going forward, several advances were made, but functional languages were still mostly confined to the academic arena with imperative programming being the more popular alternative in commercial and hobby programming.

Requirements

PHP

- PHP 5.3+ (for some libraries, a later version might be required)

Other Software:

- Extension/Library - functional-php
- Library - React/Partial
- Library - nicmart/Functionals

The functional style of programming was later brought into mainstream computer science and commercial use by the telecommunications industry which needed a fault-tolerant system.

Since the creation of Erlang by Ericsson in the late 1980s, it has been employed by various household names in a number of industry sectors. Around the same time, the Haskell programming language was born by committee, and it has since become arguably the most well-known, pure functional language.

Prerequisites

You must have access to PHP version 5.3.2 or greater and command line access to the machine in question is incredibly beneficial. When writing, I used a Debian-based machine, and a similar POSIX computer is recommended, although not required.

One of the best things you can do whilst learning is to install a decent REPL on your machine as it will make it much easier to experiment with code as you follow along. REPL stands for read-eval-print loop, and it is basically a programming environment most commonly used on the command line. It allows you to try out algorithms easily without the need for an editor or even files to contain your code. Type code into it, hit return, and your code is executed with the result printed on screen.

There are a number of good REPLs out there, and I have had success with Boris (https://github.com/d11wtq/boris) and Facebook's PHPsh (http://phpsh.org).

If you do not wish to install a REPL on your machine, then you could use http://phpepl.cloudcontrol.com or http://codepad.viper-7.com, but beware that, of course, you will not have access to install extensions or libraries. This would only become a problem for you later on, however, as in the initial stages, we will be reviewing native language features.

As we progress through more functional programming in PHP, I will suggest PHP libraries and extensions that are useful. These are either installed via Composer (http://getcomposer.org/doc/) in the case of libraries or PECL (http://pecl.php.net) for extensions. If you have not already used them, then it may pay to review them before continuing.

It goes without saying that this book is not aimed at beginner PHP developers and some object-oriented experience is assumed. Having said that, of course, this is as gentle of an introduction as possible and represents a beginner guide to functional programming in PHP.

Just What Is Functional Programming?

It is difficult to categorically define functional programming as all functional languages vary, and there is not a universally agreed-upon specification. Couple that with the fact that there are varying opinions amongst programmers as to what makes a functional language, and you have a conundrum. To confuse matters further, many languages have functional elements or primitives defined in them.

Whilst perilous, I will make an attempt at a very simplified explanation of the core tenet. Programming in a functional way is essentially coding without any assignment of values. There, I said it! Of course, there is a lot more to it, but this is the most simplistic - and also the most mind blowing - statement for those from an imperative programming background like PHP.

So just how do you get anything done in a functional style? Surely, without assignment statements nothing is possible? How do you pass values around in your programs?

The answer is incredibly simple; values can be passed from function to function as arguments and return values. Extending this idea further, we can have functions that return functions or accept functions as parameters. The more you think about it, the more powerful it becomes.

These combinations of functions express the program's intent succinctly and cleanly. The immutable constructs help to ensure that side effects cannot work their way into a functional program. Here I am referring to the avoidance of variable assignments which is the fundamental basis of imperative languages.

Humble functions are far more useful and powerful than most object-oriented PHP programmers give them credit for.

Let's See Some Code

To wipe that look of incredulity from your face, here is a simple imperative example that sums all the integers from one to ten:

```
$sum = 0;
for($i = 1; $i <= 10; $i++) {
    $sum += $i;
}
// $sum = 55
```

Versus a more functional style using PHP's `range()` function to generate an array from 1 to 10:

```
array_sum(range(1, 10)); // 55
```

Here we have hit upon a key concept and benefit of functional programming. Instead of detailing the steps required to sum the numbers, we have merely described the result we want when given a set of values.

We have also managed to avoid the use of state-tracking variables ($sum in the imperative example) and automatically divided the units of work up into reusable functions. If we need a `range()` elsewhere, we can easily reuse the same code.

Conversely in the imperative example, we are required to do all the leg work such as looping and maintaining state using variable assignments. Perhaps this could be considered as somewhat like writing a recipe where the constants are your ingredients list and the loop is equivalent to the step-by-step directions.

Continuing the food-based analogy, we might suggest that the functional example is more akin to ordering a meal at a restaurant where you simply pick from a menu. Although like a good pizzeria, you can always add more toppings yourself!

As you can probably see, functional programming and very well-designed object-oriented code can be very similar in that they both aspire to encapsulate and break down units of work into smaller reusable chunks.

Other Functional Implementations

The spectrum of languages that might consider themselves as implementing functional constructs is quite broad. In terms of pure functional languages, Haskell is possibly the most well-known. Somewhere in the middle are languages like Scala and Clojure that contain both imperative as well as functional styles.

Then much further out on the fringes, there are languages like our beloved and oft-vilified PHP, which has slowly been acquiring the basic ingredients for functional programming.

For contrast's sake, here is the same sum example in Haskell, which is as simple as:

```
sum[1..10]
```

As you can see, the syntax makes it very easy to clearly express the program in a minimal number of characters.

Commercial Uses

One oft-cited benefit or good fit for a functional approach is in the construction of domain specific languages (DSLs). The functional constructs in most languages successfully reduce the amount of low-level work required when parsing a language as built-in type handling and pattern matching enable fast and complex parsers to be written in fewer lines of code.

The advantage of this is that it greatly eases maintenance chores and makes the code simpler to understand.

A well-known commercial example of this can be found in the Functional Payout Framework for exotic trades at Barclays bank. Written in Haskell, it defines a DSL for mathematicians to create trading applications upon. The compact and flexible functional implementations allow the team to react more effectively and quickly to user requests for new features.

There were some concerns for the team at the outset of the project, chief among which was the need to interface with other legacy systems written in languages such as C. Not only was this easily completed with Haskell, but it worked out to be a bonus as it prevented tight coupling of the components.

Probably the most well-known commercial use of functional programming is the inception of the Erlang language at Ericsson, which was specifically designed to improve productivity through a high-level symbolic language. Due to the stringent reliability and concurrency demands of telecommunications, Ericsson ruled out the array of functional languages at the time with Lisp and Prolog being the front runners.

Erlang has since been adopted by many commercial users and powers numerous mission-critical pieces of hardware. It is probably the biggest success story in terms of commercial adoption and continued use in its target domain.

A more recent example comes from Twitter, which is using Scala to handle a number of key features for their social service. Whilst Scala is not a purely functional language (it has object-oriented support as well), it is certainly well-equipped to do so. Some of the features you use every day on Twitter are powered by Scala, including the store of user relationships, searching for users by name or interests, and the who to follow fuzzy suggestions that Twitter provides.

The abstractions allowed by functional programming in Scala have also meant that it is being used in many other areas as well, such as the streaming API, the kestrel queuing mechanism, and their geo systems.

What is Functional-style Programming Best For?

As you will see, anything that can be done imperatively can also be completed using functional methodologies. Although each methodology has its advantages, you can view them as simply another way of slicing the cake.

There is no golden rule that recommends functional-style programming in certain situations or object-oriented programming in others. Functional programming is not a framework or design pattern, but a Turing complete programming methodology.

To this end, as you familiarize yourself with functional programming, you will develop an innate sense of when a particular methodology is best employed to solve a problem. It is worth noting that this will be different for each programming language and that working in functional programming versus object-oriented programming in Scala is very different compared to the same in PHP.

In the PHP world, due to the bias towards object-oriented programming, functional programming is mostly used for list (array) processing, but that does not stop us from exploring more complex functional constructs as you will see further on.

The Benefits of Functional Programming

So how does removing features from your imperative language help you?

With the ever increasing popularity of functional programming, it is important to keep pace. Insights gleaned from your exploration of functional code can be applied in object-oriented programming as well.

One regularly quoted rule states that the increase in the legibility of a program improves as the level of abstraction rises by virtue of the succinct code it encourages. It is also often said that a side effect of these attributes is an increase in productivity with less typing and no global state to construct in your mind, helping to free your time for the more difficult problems.

Testing your code becomes much easier because all values are final, which means you do not have to contend with side effects. There is no particular order to maintain or global state that needs to be put into place. All you need to do is pass in the correct arguments, and you will always get the same result.

This concept is often described as referential transparency, which basically means that you can replace any function call with the value it returns, and the resulting algorithm will remain the same. Therefore instead of `range()`, we could use a static array and still get the same result:

```
array_sum(array(1, 2, 3, 4, 5, 6, 7, 8, 9, 10)); // 55
```

Substituting static values into the imperative example would be impossible (don't contort yourselves proving me wrong!), and this is where programming in a functional-style really shines. Each function, given the same input, will always return the same value.

It should not be underestimated how much easier these functions are to test than their state-filled counterparts. There is less time wasted mocking global state, and when a test fails, it will always fail, which makes it far easier to debug any test. Reproducing the bug does not require long chains of actions to surface due to the functional program's avoidance of any global state and adoption of encapsulation for its components. If a function is not returning the correct values, then it is always incorrect.

Whilst it is not usually an issue with PHP, functional programs help to prevent race conditions between threads or processes. Maintaining a functional style allows you to program these types of applications with confidence (well, almost!). The importance of parallel processing continues to grow with the advancement of computer hardware.

Computers are gaining more and more power by increasing the number of cores the central processing units contain. If your software is to take advantage of this power, then you will need to account for simultaneous processing.

This is where functional programming's abandonment of assignment statements really helps to protect you from process locking or attempting to update the same locations in memory. It also serves to make the order of execution irrelevant as without state to update, a function will always return the same value. It is when you allow state to creep into code that breaking jobs off into parallel processes falters.

Additional benefits of functional programming that do not generally apply to PHP - so we won't discuss them here - are hot code deployment and machine optimization of code.

Basics of Functional Programming in PHP

Despite the fact that PHP is inherently imperative, it can support a basic functional style of programming. To make it easier to learn, it is best to eschew some aspects of the language to emulate a purer functional one.

- Avoid changing state - even within a function.
- Attempt to keep functions to one line or as short as possible.
- Break problems down to their smallest units and turn these into reusable functions.
- Remove control statements from your code.
- As it is worth repeating; avoid state and do not use variable assignments!

You want to essentially create a little black box function that will always return the same value when given the correct arguments.

PHP has a number of language features that help to form the basis of programming in this style. Probably the most useful is the lambda function, which makes it easier to deal with code that passes functions around as variables. Additionally, language functions such as `array_map()` and `array_reduce()` are very useful for applying functions to lists of values.

There are no immutable value types or statically-typed variables in PHP so it is up to your implementation to protect your functional code from changing state.

As you begin to work in a functional way, you will need access to more primitives for the more complex operations you will encounter. Luckily, the path has been previously trodden, and there are a number of libraries that we will cover later.

Recursion
Looping with Recursion

To eliminate flow control statements such as `for`, `foreach`, and `while` in your programs, you can create loops using recursion. This is a process of repeatedly calling a function from within itself until a predetermined cut-off is reached.

A very common use of recursion in web programming revolves around printing site menu structures from content management systems, and it is also a good fit for working through file system directory trees.

```
$array = array('i', 'k', 'h', 'a', 'n', 'd', 'a');
function concat($array, $index = 0, $result = '') {
    return (array_key_exists($index, $array))
        ? concat($array, $index + 1, $result . $array[$index])
        : $result;
}
echo concat($array); // ikhanda
```

In the example above, the function recursively calls itself until it reaches the end of the array. Along the way, it joins each element of the array together.

On each iteration, the code first determines if the requested array index exists, and if it does, then it recursively calls itself (`concat()`), adds one to the index `$index`, and concatenates the current array element onto the end of the string `$result`.

When it hits the end of the array, it will return the value of `$result`, and the recursion will end.

You would never actually concatenate a string in this way, but it serves as a simple illustration of performing actions without variable assignment statements in tandem with recursive "looping".

Mutual Recursion

So far, we have covered what is known as direct recursion - where a function calls itself to create the loop. For example, if function x( ) calls x( ) itself, then it is direct recursion.

You can also implement indirect recursion (sometimes known as mutual recursion by extension) to produce a loop by creating a function, which later calls the original function again. This is where function x( ) calls function y( ), which subsequently calls x( ) again, and the loop repeats itself from there.

Head and Tail Recursion

Most recursive functions in PHP are written with head recursion, but tail recursion can be superior in some cases.

Head recursion causes the compiler to wait for a result from the called function before it can return a result of its own. On the other hand tail recursion allows the compiler to make optimizations to increase speed and reduce resource usage. Unfortunately, PHP does not take advantage of this, but it is still a good technique to master as in some cases, it can make the code clearer.

A simple example to show the two different styles with the venerable head recursion first:

```php
function head_sum($x) {
   return ($x == 1)
      ? $x
      : $x + head_sum($x - 1);
}
```

The parser will have to process all the recursive calls to head_sum( ) before it can finally add the result to $x. Tail recursion implementing the same functionality would look like the following function:

```php
function tail_sum($x, $running_total = 0) {
   return ($x == 1)
      ? $running_total
      : tail_sum($x - 1, $running_total + $x);
}
```

tail_sum( ) does not have the same problem as each iteration performs the calculation directly in line.

Unfortunately, as previously mentioned, PHP - much like Python - does not take advantage of the performance opportunities tail recursion provides.

Don't Blow the Stack

Recursive loops are powerful, but there are a few things to be mindful of when implementing them in your code. If you fail to include an exit condition, or if you choose one that is overly broad, you run the risk of unexpected behavior. Usually, this manifests itself as a stack overflow exception.

The compiler will keep looping until something stops it, so if you or the time out protections do not stop it, then the final limitation is the machine's physical resources. In this case, it will most likely be the memory limitations that you come up against first.

Bear in mind that all calls, parameters, and variable assignments in a recursive call have an impact on the amount of memory that is consumed. For example, your process will run out of memory more quickly when you have debugging code inside of it!

Map and Reduce

Map/reduce provides a simple way to create elegant code solutions to complex list processing operations, and it has proven useful for high-availability, large-scale processing. You may have heard of Hadoop, CouchDB, and similar NoSQL solutions implementing map/ reduce - not to mention Google's indexing algorithm. Using `array_map()` and `array_reduce()`, it is also possible to exploit these techniques with PHP.

Map

Map iterates over a set of data to produce a new list of values by applying a function to each item in the list. Most `for` and `foreach` loops can easily be replaced with a call to `array_map()`. The key difference is that it separates the computational function from the loop itself.

Of course, this easily lends itself to code re-use where you may need to apply the same operation to a list in a different context.

On the other hand, in PHP at least, it is slightly slower to use `array_map()` than employing `foreach`, but unless you are the kind of developer to fret over micro-optimizations, the difference is negligible.

```php
function times_two($val) { return $val * 2; }
$array = array(1, 2, 3, 4, 5);
$results = array_map('times_two', $array);
// array(2, 4, 6, 8, 10)
```

An interesting thought for you now - that list could contain functions and not just primitive values. You could use `array_map()` to execute all the functions contained in an array and return all their values, for example.

Reduce

Reduce, on the other hand, loops over a list to collapse or combine the values therein into one final value by applying the same processing function to each value in the list. This operation is sometimes known as a fold function, and the PHP `array_reduce()` function can be considered analogous to a left fold.

In the following reduce example, you can see that it operates on a list of integers and adds each element to a total. This is an iterative process that works upon one element in the array at a time.

```php
function sum($result, $val) { return $result + $val; }
$array = array(1, 2, 3, 4, 5);
$results = array_reduce($array, 'sum', 0);
// 15
```

In Harmony

Of course, these two techniques can be combined to great effect. If you were to have a set containing a list of documents, you could use a mapping function to iterate through each one and calculate its file size on disk. In addition, it would be great to know the total file size so you could use a reduce function to iterate over the file sizes and sum them up, reusing the sum() function created above.

```php
function get_filesize($path) { return filesize($path); }
array_reduce(
    array_map('get_filesize', $array_of_file_paths),
    'sum',
    0
);
```

Here you have seen `array_reduce()` directly working upon the array result returned by `array_map()`. It is a very simple example, but you can use these two operations to easily work through lists, large or small.

You may have noticed a highly irritating fact about PHP's implementation of these two little functions - they don't maintain the same parameter order! Reduce accepts the collection (or array) first and then the callback function, whereas map is the opposite way around.

Filter

With the help of filtering, you can return a result set from a list of values by applying a callback function known as a predicate to each item in the list. The predicate will return either a Boolean false to remove the record or true to keep the list item in the result set. Whilst this may sound a little complicated, in practice, it makes cleaning lists a breeze.

```php
function filter_callback($val) { return ($val % 2 === 0); }
array_filter(
    array(1, 2, 3, 4, 5),
    'filter_callback'
);
// array(2, 4);
```

In the preceding example, we are applying a filter callback to a simple list of integers. The callback itself checks if the supplied number is cleanly divisible by two, which is a simple way of detecting if the value is an even or an odd number.

`array_filter()` is then used to iterate over the array of integers and apply the callback to each value therein. This results in a new array being returned that contains only the even numbers, being two and four in this case.

λ

It is often helpful to declare a function without a formal identifier or function name. Now this may sound silly, but you are probably already doing it when passing functions in as callback parameters. A good example in PHP is the venerable `spl_autoload_register()` which takes a function as its first parameter:

```php
$lambda_function = function($class_name) {
    include 'classes/' . $class_name . '.class.php';
};
spl_autoload_register($lambda_function);
```

These functions are often referred to as lambda (λ) functions or anonymous functions interchangeably. As you can see, they can be assigned to variables, but equally, they can be defined directly in the parameter of the receiving function (in this case, `spl_autoload_register()`):

```php
spl_autoload_register(function($class_name) {
    include 'classes/' . $class_name . '.class.php';
});
```

If you have some experience with JavaScript, then this pattern will look very familiar.

Forgive the hyperbole, but just about every piece of functional code ever written makes use of lambda functions, and they are an important building block to add to your tool kit and should be mastered before continuing.

Closures

Closures are an important feature of any functional language and have been deemed so useful that a lot of imperative languages now also support their use. PHP is no exception to this with support for closures introduced in PHP 5.3.

They can be used to transport code and data around as a package. It could be considered that a closure represents a similar role in functional programming as objects perform in object-oriented programming. In fact in PHP, creating a closure actually returns an instance of the internal Closure class.

```php
$add_value = 10;
$closure = function($param) use ($add_value) {
    return $param + $add_value;
};
echo $closure(2); // 12
echo $closure(60); // 70
```

You may be thinking that in the example above, it looks just like a lambda function. So what is the difference? Looking a little more closely, you will notice that an additional use clause has been added after the function declaration - use ($add_value). This structure makes it possible to pass a value from the parent scope into a closure.

Importantly, the variables passed into the closure with the use statement are set at the point of the closure's definition and not when the closure is later called.

This is useful for values that you need access to on every call of the function and that will not change after the closure's definition. Commonly, it is implemented when you want to pass other closures or lambda functions into the closure you are defining.

```php
$array = array(12345, 'abcde');
$lambda = function($value) { return md5($value); };
$closure = function($value) use ($lambda) {
   return 'MD5 Hash: ' . $lambda($value);
};
$result = array_map($closure, $array);
// array(
//     "MD5 Hash: 827ccb0eea8a706c4c34a16891f84e7b",
//     "MD5 Hash: ab56b4d92b40713acc5af89985d4b786"
// )
```

Here you can see a lambda function being passed into a closure which is then called upon each element in $array using array_map( ) to create an MD5 hash for each value in the array.

Higher Order Functions

Instead of using control statements, functional programming makes use of higher order functions which form expressions. Higher order functions are those that take other functions as arguments and/or return a function.

See the code sample below for a very contrived example that exhibits some aspects of this paradigm. We are passing in a function as an argument and returning a function from get_algorithm( ). The function it returns will be executed against each item in the array by array_map( ).

```php
$data = array(1, 2, 3, 4, 5, 6, 7, 8, 9, 10);
function get_algorithm($rand_seed_fnc) {
    return (odd_even($rand_seed_fnc())) ?
        function($value) {
            return $value * $value;
        } :
        function($value) use ($rand_seed_fnc) {
            return ($value * $value / $rand_seed_fnc()) + 10;
        };
}
function odd_even($value) {
    return ($value % 2 === 0);
}
$rand_seed_fnc = function() { return rand(); };
$results = array_map(get_algorithm($rand_seed_fnc), $data);
```

This example shows how functions can easily be reused and passed around to create richer algorithms. This is merely an extension of the functionality we saw earlier whilst exploring the spl_autoload_register( ) examples in the lambda functions section.

You can also create more useful expressions with higher order functions with techniques of currying, composition, and partial function application, all of which will be addressed in the upcoming sections.

Partial Function Application (PFA)

Sometimes when you are operating on a list of values, it can be helpful to apply a function to it without knowing all the parameter values at the point of definition. For example, imagine a function that gets the first character of each item in the list:

```
$first_char = function($string) {
    return substr($string, 0, 1);
};
$mapped = array_map($first_char, array('foo', 'bar', 'baz'));
// array('f', 'b', 'b')
```

Firstly, we create a new anonymous function, $first_char, which calls substr() and sets two of that function's parameters to the defaults of 0 and 1. This partial function is then applied to a list of words by PHP's array_map(). Whilst this solves a problem, it is not the most elegant of code and basically boils down to function wrapping.

There is a PHP library called React/Partial (https://github.com/reactphp/partial) which makes this process easier and adds syntactic sugar to the exercise.

To make this clearer, here is an example of the React\Partial function in use from their documentation:

```
use React\Partial;
$first_char = Partial\bind('substr', Partial\...(), 0, 1);
$mapped = array_map($first_char, array('foo', 'bar', 'baz'));
// array('f', 'b', 'b')
```

Partial\...() is a placeholder that will be replaced by the value passed in at run time, which in this example is each item in the list array('foo', 'bar', 'baz').

At the time of writing, there is also a PHP RFC (https://wiki.php.net/rfc/currying) for adding partial function application to the core of PHP using a new `curry` keyword and the same UTF-8 ellipsis as React/Partial for the placeholder. Before going further though, I must address that name - curry - as it is not actually currying, but partial function application.

The two terms refer to two distinct processes for reducing the number of parameters a function accepts, but they are often conflated. It cannot be denied that the term curry is snappier than partial function application despite the potential for confusion. For now, we will gloss over it, but in the next section, you will see some true currying.

As an aside; to learn more about PHP's RFC process, I would recommend a quick look through Christopher Jones's blog post: https://blogs.oracle.com/opal/entry/the_mysterious_php_rfc_process.

Currying

So what is it really? Currying relies on the principle that it is possible to treat almost any function as a partial function of just one argument. To facilitate the currying process, the return values of the functions are actually functions themselves. Each parameter passed to the original function will become a function that is returned.

With closure support now available in PHP, it is possible to emulate currying. So let us step through a manually curried example to give you an idea of what is happening internally.

```php
$x = function($start) {
    return function($length) use ($start) {
        return function($string) use ($start, $length) {
            return substr($string, $start, $length);
        };
    };
};
```

As you can see, this is very similar to the code example from the partial function application examples earlier. Believe it or not, when this code is run, it will achieve the same result. In a more formula-orientated sense, our function has gone from:

```
((a, b, c) -> d)
```

to:

```
(a -> b -> c -> d)
```

So what is the advantage of this over a partial function application? You can form many partial functions at run time and at any stage in the function chain. Partial function applications on the other hand define the functions "partialness" at declaration.

With that out of the way, we can get on with using our manually curried example.

```
$a = $x(0);
$b = $a(1);
$b('foo'); // 'f'
```

Firstly, we pass in the character offset we want substr() to use by feeding 0 to $x(). Next up, we set the length of the string to return by calling $a(1). You will probably have noted that $a() is the return value from the previous line of code. Finally, we can pass in a string for the code to operate on for the return value of the last line of code ($b()).

We can infer from this that $b() is the same as $first_char() in our partial function application example. If we want to get the first character from another string, then we could just call:

```
$b('bar'); // 'b'
$b('wena'); // 'w'
```

However, if we later wanted to get the first two characters, then we could run the following code:

```
$c = $a(2);
$c('foo'); // 'fo'
$c('bar'); // 'ba'
$c('wena'); // 'we'
```

Here we are generating a new function ($c()) by setting the length to 2 so that our new partial function returns the first two letters of the supplied string. Once again, as you can see, it is using the return value of $x(0) (a function) to pass in the length required.

All well and good you might say, but awfully verbose. The basic mechanics in the code samples can be automated using the curry functionality in the nicmart/Functionals library, like so:

```
use Functionals\Functionals;
$x = Functionals::curry(function($start, $length, $string) {
   return substr($string, $start, $length);
});
$a = $x(0);
$b = $a(1);
$b('foo'); // 'f'
$c = $a(2);
$c('foo'); // 'fo'
```

Elfet/Functional and funktional also have the concept of currying, but I prefer the implementation in nicmart/Functionals. The details of the libraries mentioned here are covered in more depth further on.

There is no technical reason or special meaning to be gleaned from the name of this functional methodology, but you are probably wondering where the term currying does come from. Well, it has nothing to do with the delicious food of the same name - although every time you curry a function, you may experience pangs of hunger. Just me? I doubt that!

The technique is in fact named after a mathematician named Haskell Curry - who incidentally gives his name to the Haskell programming language, among others as well. There is some controversy around this naming as it is widely understood that Moses Schönfinkel laid the ground work for the combinatory logic, and therefore, currying should perhaps be known as Schönfinkelization.

Whatever you choose to call it, it is a very powerful technique as demonstrated by Haskell (the programming language, not the man) making use of currying for all functions that accept more than one parameter.

Composing

It can often be helpful to combine functions to create reusable and more complex functions. The return value of each function is passed into the next, and the result of the last function is the final value returned. In mathematics and computer science, this process is known as composition.

PHP does not currently understand function composition, so we must define a new function to implement the logic:

```php
function compose($a, $b) {
    return function() use ($a, $b) {
        $args = func_get_args();
        return $b(call_user_func_array($a, $args));
    };
}
```

This function accepts two functions as parameters, which are then composed together by $b() being passed the result of function $a(). The compose() function also handles applying the supplied arguments to $a(). It is important that the return value/type from $a() is expected as an input parameter to $b(), or you will trigger a PHP error. Should you need to pass multiple arguments from $a() to $b(), then you will need to return an array as the result of $a().

Now, let's put this composer into action:

```php
$a = function($val) { return str_word_count($val); };
$b = function($val) { return $val - 2; };
$c = compose($a, $b);
$c('Here is some text to word count.'); // 5
```

In this contrived example, you can see two functions being composed with the first obtaining a simple word count from a supplied string and the second subtracting two from any integer passed into it. When the two functions are composed, the resulting function is $c(), which takes one string parameter and returns an integer value.

It is possible to call any object that implements the `__invoke()` magic method as a function, and this process is commonly known in the PHP world as a functor. In effect, the class instance becomes a closure when called in this way.

```php
class SumFunctor {
    public function __invoke($x, $y) {
        return $x + $y;
    }
}
$SumFunctor = new SumFunctor;
$SumFunctor(5, 10); // 15
```

There are a number of reasons that you might consider implementing your functions in this way. The major advantages are that a closure becomes much easier to reuse, and it affords the ability to be more specific when type hinting.

It should be noted that this functionality is not actually a functor as defined by category theory and a more accurate computing-based term would be a function object. In category theory, a functor is a mapping between two categories where the structure of the category being mapped is preserved.

Having said that, the term functor is used to describe a number of differing techniques across languages, and PHP is siding with C++ in this respect.

Memoization

The process of result caching can help to speed up expensive operations by returning a pre-chewed set of data. Fetching the values from a cache allows an application to skip the slow running code and still return the correct results. The secret sauce of PHP's memoization is the `static` keyword, which effectively pins a variable to a resource in memory. Any time that resource is updated in the same PHP process, the new value is recalled on the next invocation of the function.

```php
$a = function($value) {
    static $array = array();
    return empty($array)
        ? $array = get_some_really_expensive_data()
        : $array;
};
```

This operation can be simplified by using the `F\memoize()` function of the functional-php library (discussed more in-depth later):

```php
use Functional as F;
$callback_function = function($arg) {
    return get_some_really_expensive_data($arg);
};
$result = F\memoize($callback_function, array('php'));
```

A good example of where this might be useful is in caching the parsing of large documents into a hash or limiting calls to a database for a widely-reused function.

Helpful Libraries

So now that you have seen some techniques for manipulating data in a functional way, you are probably wondering which primitives and higher order functions PHP has to offer in the default installation. Unfortunately, the answer is not many, although this is changing all the time as the language evolves.

To help fill this void, Lars Strojny has created a PECL extension called functional-php (https://github.com/lstrojny/functional-php). If you are unable to install PECL extensions on your host, then there is even a pure PHP userland version of the library available.

Many, if not all, of the functions are inspired by implementations of functional primitives in other languages such as JavaScript and Scala. Unfortunately at this stage, there is no implementation of any sorting functionality in the extension or library, but it is on the road map for the project.

Not only does functional-php have handy primitives, but it also unifies the interface for operating on lists. All functions have the same order of parameters, so no more hassle remembering whether it is the collection or callback that comes first!

Another very handy feature is that in addition to arrays, its functions can operate on any object that implements PHP's `Traversable` interface.

It is important to try to keep the API consistent with your own code and when importing other functional libraries to facilitate easier future maintenance.

Additionally, there is the Underscore.php library written by Brian Haveri http://brianhaveri.github.com/Underscore.php/, which is a pure PHP set of functional primitives that cover a lot of the same ground as functional-php. There are one or two additional features such as `__::sortBy` and `__::compose()`, so you may want to use the two projects in tandem. Similar libraries include Nicolò Martini's Functionals (https://github.com/nicmart/Functionals) and funktional (http://code.google.com/p/funktional/) written by Fabio Testolin.

As previously mentioned in the partial function application section,

React/Partial (https://github.com/reactphp/partial) is a very handy library to have available to your projects for partial function application syntactic sugar.

Library Installation

The main library that will be used throughout the following code samples is functional-php, and it can either be installed as a PHP/PECL extension or as a userland PHP library. If you have the option, then I would suggest the extension route, but if you cannot build or install extensions on your server, then you can use the library. For initial playing around, you may find it easier to opt for the library route as well. If you are following along on a Windows machine, then install it as a library.

If you have chosen to install it as a library rather than an extension, please skip to the "Other PHP Libraries" section heading below.

functional-php

The functional-php extension must be built from source as the PECL releases are old and missing the latest features so the first thing to do is to download a ZIP file of the source from GitHub (https://github.com/lstrojny/functional-php/archive/master.zip).

Extract the ZIP file to a suitable temporary folder somewhere, and then change directories into it. From inside the functional-php projects root folder, execute the following commands:

```
phpize
./configure
make
sudo make install
```

Once the extension is built using any of the aforementioned methods, you will also need to enable it in the php.ini file by adding:

```
extension=functional.so
```

It should be noted here that if you are using this extension with a website rather than on the PHP CLI, then you will need to restart your webserver for the new PHP configuration to take effect.

You should remove the functional-php line from the composer.json requirements described in the next section before installing the dependencies if you have already installed functional-php via the extension method described above. If you fail to do this, the userland PHP library version will still be installed, though it will be ignored harmlessly in deference to the PHP extension.

Other PHP Libraries

With the exception of functional-php, all the aforementioned libraries are supplied as userland PHP code allowing them to be installed via the usual methods such as downloading a tarball. However, with the help of the Composer dependency management system and the Packagist repository, you can make the process a lot simpler.

To get started, you will need to download the Composer phar (PHP archive) file from the Packagist website to the root directory of your project, which on POSIX machines looks like this:

```
curl -s http://getcomposer.org/installer | php
```

Also in the base folder of the application, you should define a JSON object in the composer.json file to configure the dependencies of your project. To make this process quicker and easier, see the code sample below which contains the full composer.json requirements file for all the aforementioned libraries. Should you not wish to install a library, you can simply remove it from the list. For more information on the requirements file format, please see the Composer documentation (http://getcomposer.org/doc/).

```
{
    "repositories": [
        {
            "type": "package",
            "package": {
                "name": "brianhaveri/Underscore.php",
                "version": "dev-master",
                "dist": {
                    "url": "https://github.com/brianhaveri/
                        Underscore.php/archive/master.zip",
                    "type": "zip"
                },
                "autoload": {
                    "classmap": ["underscore.php"]
                }
            }
        }
    ],
    "require": {
        "react/partial": "~2.0",
        "nicmart/functionals": "dev-master",
        "brianhaveri/Underscore.php": "dev-master",
        "lstrojny/functional-php": "dev-master",
        "phpoption/phpoption": "1.*"
    }
}
```

Once you have decided which libraries to install and have amended your `composer.json` file appropriately, you can install them with a single command:

```
php composer.phar install
```

Should a project you depend upon be updated with changes at a later date, you can simply call:

```
php composer.phar update
```

Now, in your project's bootstrap or index file, you can include all of the Composer/Packagist supplied dependencies by simply adding the following line of PHP code:

```
require 'vendor/autoload.php';
```

If you are using version control (and you should be), then you will want to remember to ignore/exclude `composer.lock`, `composer.phar`, and the `vendor` directory before committing.

Implementing the Theory 16

The Setup

Let's run through a few examples of how these features could potentially be combined to assist in reporting for a vehicle repair business. Please see the code sample below for the base set of data that all of these operations will be working upon.

```php
// Odometer: distance covered by a vehicle in miles or
//     kilometers
// Rego: Vehicle registration or plate number
// Hours: Time spent working on the vehicle
// Parts cost: Charge to the customer for the cost of parts
$service_logs = array(
    array('rego' => 'DG44-001', 'odometer' => 91234,
        'hours' => 0.36, 'parts_cost' => 31.99),
    array('rego' => 'LJ32-091', 'odometer' => 7986,
        'hours' => 1, 'parts_cost' => 278.54),
    array('rego' => 'DG44-001', 'odometer' => 58709,
        'hours' => 3, 'parts_cost' => 1002.29),
    array('rego' => 'DG44-001', 'odometer' => 23487,
        'hours' => 10, 'parts_cost' => 3932.96),
);
$charge_per_hour = 120;
$overhead_per_hour = 10;
```

The initial setup is simple enough, so let's go ahead and pull in the vendor autoloader from Composer and the functional-php namespace:

```php
require_once 'vendor/autoload.php';
use Functional as F;
```

Another small piece of housekeeping also needs to be completed so that we can make a more functional uasort() available to our program as unfortunately, PHP edits the array in place and does not return the sorted array, but a Boolean value. This, of course, violates our pact to ensure all data in our functional program is immutable so this wrapping function goes part of the way to rectifying that.

```php
function functional_sort($collection, $callback) {
    uasort($collection, $callback);
    return $collection;
}
```

Sort and Pluck

Let's keep it simple for the first example by pulling out the highest vehicle mileage in the records. A handy hint for you when reading nested function calls like this is that it is best to read from the inside out.

```php
$highest_odometer_reading = F\first(
    functional_sort(
        F\pluck($service_logs, 'odometer'),
        function($a, $b) {
            return ($a < $b);
        }
    )
);
```

From the inside out: firstly F\pluck() is called to return an array of the mileage elements from the service logs. At this point, the value that the program is operating on becomes:

```php
array(91234, 7986, 58709, 23487);
```

This functionality will also be available in PHP 5.5 under the name array_column() as the related RFC (https://wiki.php.net/rfc/array_column) was voted through.

However, let's get back to our odometer reading example. The next function to operate on the service logs is a sorting algorithm using the custom functional_sort() which we defined earlier. Then finally, F\first() grabs the top record off the stack and assigns the value 91234 to the $highest_odometer_reading variable.

Reduction

Cutting the data another way makes it possible to calculate the total profit that the garage has made on the service work it has performed for customers. Again, see the first code sample in this chapter for the origin of the $charge_per_hour and $overhead_per_hour variables used in the algorithm closure.

```
$profit = F\reduce_left(
    $service_logs,
    function($value, $index, $collection, $result)
        use ($charge_per_hour, $overhead_per_hour) {
        return $result +
            ($value['hours'] * $charge_per_hour) -
            ($value['hours'] * $overhead_per_hour) +
            $value['parts_cost'];
    }
);
```

The code is simply using a reduce to go through each service record, calculating the profit on each job and adding it to the accumulating $result variable. When the value is finally assigned to $profit, it is a single float of 6825.38. You may have noticed this function does not take into account the cost to the business of the parts (in the example, parts_cost is the cost for the customer) - this is just to simplify the example code.

The F\reduce_left() function is functionally equivalent to PHP's native array_reduce(), except like the rest of functional-php, it can operate on objects implementing Traversable. The library also makes F\reduce_right() available with the difference being that it begins reducing from the last element in the collection whereas F\reduce_left() begins with the first element in the collection.

It is possible to make some improvements to the program by factoring out the profit calculation code into a separate closure that can be reused:

```
$calculate_profit = function($hours, $parts_cost)
    use ($charge_per_hour, $overhead_per_hour) {
    return ($hours * $charge_per_hour) -
        ($hours * $overhead_per_hour) +
        $parts_cost;
};
```

Now we can tighten up the collection processing functionality as well by using three functions from functional-php.

```
$profit = F\sum(
    F\zip(
        F\pluck($service_logs, 'hours'),
        F\pluck($service_logs, 'parts_cost'),
        $calculate_profit
    )
);
```

Beginning with the inner functions first and working outwards, F\pluck() is used to pull the hours and parts_cost elements from each service log record. F\zip() is then employed to combine the two resulting arrays using the $calculate_profit closure as the combining operation and returns an array containing the profit subtotal for every service log record. These subtotals are then totted up into one final profit total, which is then returned as a float from F\sum() and assigned to $profit.

Filtering with Partials

Often, customers will want to obtain a complete list of the service history for their vehicle or a vehicle they have recently purchased. With the assistance of some filtering combined with a sorting algorithm, it is possible to return an array of service logs ordered by odometer reading for a particular vehicle registration number.

```
function get_by_rego($service_logs, $rego) {
    return functional_sort(
        F\filter($service_logs, function($value) use ($rego) {
            return ($rego == $value['rego']);
        }),
        function($a, $b) {
            return ($a['odometer'] > $b['odometer']);
        }
    );
}
```

Initially, the service logs are filtered down to only those that matched the vehicle registration that has been passed in using F\filter() with a callback closure function. The resulting array is then ordered by each service record's odometer reading with an ascending sort.

To make it easier to use this function, we can bind the `$service_logs` variable to the function using the React/Partial function application library.

```
use React\Partial;
$get_by_rego = Partial\bind('get_by_rego', $service_logs,
    Partial\...());
```

It is then possible to easily obtain the records for a vehicle registration number by calling `$get_by_rego()`.

```
$get_by_rego('DG44-001');
// array(
//     array("rego" => "DG44-001", "odometer" => 23487,
//           "hours" => 10, "parts_cost" => 3932.96),
//     array("rego" => "DG44-001", "odometer" => 58709,
//           "hours" => 3, "parts_cost" => 1002.29),
//     array("rego" => "DG44-001", "odometer" => 91234,
//           "hours" => 0.36, "parts_cost" => 31.99)
// )
```

This could also be implemented using functional-php's `F\group()` function to first group all the records by a vehicle registration number instead of `F\filter()`, but this would be less efficient in terms of memory usage as the array would be much larger.

From these highly contrived examples, you can see some of the ways that functional primitives and higher order functions can be combined to achieve business goals. They also highlight the advantages of keeping functions simple and confined to answering one problem each, thereby facilitating their eventual combined use and re-use.

17

Advances in PHP

Advances in PHP 5.4

With the introduction of PHP 5.4, new features have been added that make programming in a functional style easier. The first of these additions is the `callable` type hint (http://php.net/manual/en/language.types.callable.php). It can be specified for one or more parameters in a function's signature, ensuring that the passed value is a callback. The specification of the callback can be a string containing the name of a PHP function, a lambda function or closure, array class notation, or a static method as a string representation.

```php
function callable_func($collection, callable $callback) {
    return array_map($callback, $collection);
}
$seed_data = array('BIZA', 'IBIZO', 'LAMI');
$result  = callable_func($seed_data, 'strtolower');
$result2 = callable_func($seed_data, function($value) {
    return ucwords(strtolower($value));
});
```

Next up is a handy addition to make defining arrays a little easier on the keyboard, which has been snappily named: short array syntax. It works just like this:

```php
$seed_data = [ 'BIZA', 'IBIZO', 'LAMI' ];
$key_data  = [
    'call' => 'BIZA',
    'name' => 'IBIZO',
    'mine' => 'LAMI'
];
```

Isn't it annoying when you cannot skip straight to a certain array element returned from a function call? With array dereferencing now in the PHP core, a pet peeve of mine - for as long as I can remember - has now been fixed.

```
function get_map() {
    return [ 'version' => '1.2.4', 'build' => '20151012' ];
}
echo get_map()['build']; // 20151012
```

In a similar vein, you can now also access class members on instantiation - although unfortunately, it is not possible to call functors in this way:

```
(new Foo)->bar(); // calls the bar() method successfully
(new SumFunctor)(5, 10); // throws a parse error :(
// the closest you can get is:
(new SumFunctor)->__invoke(5, 10);
```

There is currently an open feature request in PHP's bug tracker (https://bugs.php.net/bug.php?id=63253), and there is an open pull request which is hopefully destined for PHP 5.6 (https://github.com/php/php-src/pull/301) that will fix this.

While not strictly applicable to functional programming, there is one further implementation detail supported by closures in PHP 5.4 which deserves a quick mention. You can bind a class to a closure instance to make the class available as $this within the closure. This saves you from having to pass in the context via a use statement incorporating the $this - $that dance.

Advances in PHP 5.5

With 5.5 there is a new list of features available. Here are my picks for functional programming.

Generators are simple constructs that allow you to bring the lazy loading style functionality to building arrays such as those returned by range().

Instead of building the whole array in one hit up front, it will generate the next item just in time for the next iteration, which results in significant memory savings. Here is an example taken from the PHP manual and using the functional-php class introduced in Chapter 16.

```
function xrange($start, $limit, $step = 1) {
    for ($i = $start; $i <= $limit; $i += $step) {
        yield $i;
    }
}
echo F\sum(xrange(1, 10)); // 55
```

The empty() language construct can now take function return values directly:

```php
function another_function() {
    return empty(some_function());
}
```

It will now also be possible to dereference arrays and string literals directly:

```php
echo [ 1, 2, 3, 4, 5 ][2]; // 3
echo 'ikhanda'[4]; // n
```

As previously mentioned, PHP will also receive array pluck functionality in the form of the array_column() function.

Further into the Future

Whilst it is difficult to tell what will be accepted into future versions of PHP beyond that of the RFCs that have completed votes against them, there has been some discussion on the PHP internals list (http://markmail.org/thread/uvendztpe2rrwiif) of adding list comprehension functions. It would be quite a boon for PHP were these features to be added to the language so I will cover them here in the hope that greater awareness leads to greater demand!

Nikita Popov has provided a patch (https://github.com/nikic/php-src/tree/addListComprehensions) that uses the following syntax to describe a list comprehension:

```php
// get a list of registration numbers
$registration_numbers = [foreach ($service_logs as $log)
    yield $log['rego']
];
// this equivalent to the following code
$registration_numbers = array();
foreach($service_logs as $log) {
    $registration_numbers[] = $log['rego'];
}
```

It would also be possible to filter records to return only records that have the registration number of DG44-001:

```php
$filtered_records =
    [foreach ($service_logs as $log) if ($log == 'DG44-001')
        yield $log
    ];
```

The final advantage is the ability for the system to work on nested `foreach` statements like so (example taken directly from Nikita's introductory email):

```php
$a_list = array('A', 'B');
$b_list = array(1, 2);
$combinations = [foreach ($a_list as $a)
      foreach ($b_list as $b)
      yield array($a, $b)
   ];
// array(
//     array('A', 1),
//     array('A', 2),
//     array('B', 1),
//     array('B', 2)
// )
```

As you can see, this is a powerful feature that would make operating on arrays in PHP far easier. Given their succinct nature coupled with a stateless operation, they would make a good addition to the functional programming toolkit.

Nikita does not stop there, though, but goes further with another RFC that defines syntax for variadic functions in PHP 5.6 (https://wiki.php.net/rfc/variadics). This is a handy feature that adds a symbol to a function that can take unlimited arguments and replaces the annoyances required when using the current `func_get_args()` method.

```php
function prln($title) {
   $messages = array_slice(func_get_args(), 1);
   echo "$title: " . implode(', ', $messages);
}
```

This becomes the far simpler and more obvious:

```php
function prln($title, ...$messages) {
   echo "$title: " . implode(', ', $messages);
}
```

The Future Looks Good

As PHP moves into the future, it looks like the new versions are adding more features and functions that should help to make functional programming a solid reality in PHP.

Handling Your NULLs

18

There are a number of functions in PHP - and I am sure many more in the legacy userland code you work on - that return NULL when no record can be found, for example. When you then call that function, you cannot be sure if it will return a record as you expect or a null value, which violates the principle that a function should always return the same type for it to be handled in the same way.

We have previously implemented the array_reduce() function, and it serves again as a great example. When it is fed an empty array, it will return NULL. Say the result of our reduce operation were to be passed into a function expecting to receive an integer; then it would trigger an error from PHP's parser.

There are a few ways to handle these null values and protect your code from unforeseen errors.

In the case of array_reduce(), you can simply set an initial value as the third parameter to the function. This initial value will be returned if the input array is empty; otherwise, it will be used as the base value to add each reduce operation to.

If you do not have control over the code you are calling or you are implementing a function that does not allow for a default return value, then you can make use of the following two techniques.

The first is a very simple solution using the implicit return value property of PHP's ternary operator. This works by leaving the second expression in the ternary operation empty like so:

```
$var = get_record() ?: array();
```

This code will assign the return value of get_record() to $var unless it is null in which case it will assign the empty array specified as the third expression of the ternary in the example.

Now I must address a minor matter I glossed over for brevity's sake in the previous sentence. It is not only a return value of NULL that will trigger a replacement. PHP also considers the following values to evaluate to false:

- false, of course
- an integer set to 0
- a float of 0.0
- an empty string or the string value "0"
- arrays containing no elements
- SimpleXML objects created from empty tags
- values of NULL

What if you only want to replace NULL values? Unfortunately, you are out of luck with the native PHP offerings, but Johannes Schmitt has written the php-option library (https://github.com/schmittjoh/php-option). His library ports functionality similar to Scala's Option values (http://www.scala-lang.org/api/current/index.html#scala.Option) to PHP.

Fortunately, it allows you to be more specific about when to supply a replacement value, such as in this example which only replaces a value of NULL or an integer:

```php
function get_safe_record() {
    $record = get_record();
    return (!is_null($record) && !is_int($record))
        ? new \PhpOption\Some($record)
        : \PhpOption\None::create();
}
$record = get_safe_record()
    ->getOrElse(array());
```

If you only want to protect code from null values, then you can use the fromValue() static method instead like so:

```php
function get_safe_record() {
    return \PhpOption\Option::fromValue(get_record());
}
```

There is another advantage of this library in that you can chain calls to orElse() so that the code may try multiple alternatives to resolve the null return value.

```
$record = get_cached_record()
    ->orElse(get_api_record())
    ->orElse(create_new_record());
```

This example simulates talking to a set of records available via a third-party API. If it cannot find a cached record, then it will attempt to pull it across from the API. Were that to also fail, then it will create a new record and return it instead.

As you can see, these techniques can be employed to assist us in our goal of avoiding flow control and assignment statements like those in this imperative example:

```
function get_safe_record() {
    $record = get_cached_record();
    if(is_null($record)) {
        $record = get_api_record();
    }
    if(is_null($record)) {
        $record = create_new_record();
    }
    return $record;
}
```

Furthermore, if the code you are talking to requires you to instantiate objects, then you can employ lazy loading via php-option's getOrCall() method to stop PHP from creating the instance until it is actually required.

```
$record = get_record()->getOrCall(function() {
    return ORM::for_table('records');
});
```

Dealing with null values in PHP can be tricky, but with the help of these patterns, you can mitigate the errors that would otherwise interrupt your code or require flow control statements and defensive programming.

19

More Functors

We have already seen PHP's functors use the `__invoke()` method in a class, but as we also discovered, this is merely an object function and not a true functor. To understand what constitutes a functor, we must delve a little deeper into the theory. Simple values can have a function applied to them with little fuss:

```
function x($v) { return $v * 2; }
echo x(2); // 4
```

That goes as expected, but what if this value were stored in a context? To make it easier to picture this, imagine that a context acts much like having a value wrapped up inside a box. This context will affect the result of any function called against the value it contains.

Of course, our function `x()` does not expect anything but a simple numeric value, and if the value has been bound up into a context, it can no longer be directly applied in the same manner.

To facilitate this, you will need a universal way of calling functions against these bound values. In Haskell, this is the job of a function called `fmap`, but in PHP, you must write your own code to emulate the functionality.

So the following is a very simple PHP functor that matches the code we saw earlier:

```
class x {
   public function __invoke($v) {
      return $v * 2;
   }
}
$x = new x;
echo $x(2); // 4
```

To add a context to the input value, we need to declare a simple type class, which will wrap up the value in a box (see Figure 19.1):

```
class Just {
   public $value = null;
   public function __construct($value) {
      $this->value = $value;
   }
}
```

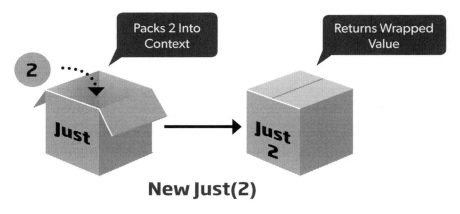

New Just(2)

Figure 19.1: Wrapping the Value in Just

If we now try to apply the PHP functor to this wrapped value, we will witness an almighty crunch resulting in a PHP notice:

```
echo $x(new Just(2));
// PHP Notice: Object of class Just could not be converted
// to int
```

To fix this, we must create an emulation of Haskell's fmap( ) function in PHP (see Figure 19.2 [next page]), which is actually quite simple:

```
function fmap($function, $just) {
   return $function($just->value);
}
echo fmap($x, new Just(2)); // 4
```

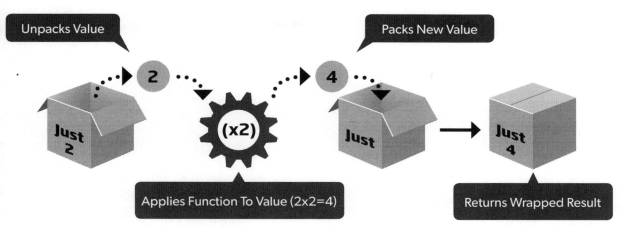

Figure 19.2 : Applying a Function to a Just

The beauty of fmap( ) is that it knows how to unpack the value from its context before applying a function to it.

So far so good. However, functors should also return a wrapped value back so we need to modify fmap( ) slightly:

```
function fmap($function, $just) {
    return new Just($function($just->value));
}
$result = fmap($x, new Just(2)); // Just(4)
```

So far, the code we have seen is not exactly universal as I had promised - just try applying fmap( ) to a list of values! To make it easier for fmap( ), we must define some more data types and specify how fmap( ) is to be applied to each one. To start with, we will create an interface that our type classes will implement:

```
interface FunctorInterface {
    /**
     * Defines how fmap should apply this data type
     * @param callable $function
     * @return FunctorInterface
     */
    public function __invoke($function);
}
```

Defining the interface makes it possible to type check using PHP's `instanceOf`, and to make it easier on yourself, define an abstract class for the type classes to extend:

```php
abstract class Functor implements FunctorInterface {
    protected $container = null;
    public function __construct($data = null) {
        $this->set($data);
    }
    public function get() {
        return $this->container;
    }
    public function set($value) {
        $this->container = $value;
    }
}
```

As you can see, this is really quite a simple container class that stores a value in `$container`. Next up, we can improve upon the earlier Just type class with the following code:

```php
class Just extends Functor {
    public function __invoke($function) {
        return new Just($function($this->container));
    }
}
```

You may be wondering why I have defined both an abstract class and an interface. This is a personal preference for a couple of reasons, stemming from the fact that I firmly believe that only interfaces should be used to form contracts and type hints.

This allows anyone to replace the abstract with one of their own and just implement the interface, so your code will still work. The second and most useful part of this is that PHP can implement many interfaces, but it can only extend one class. By not forcing an implementer to extend your abstract, they may inherit from any class they desire.

This is the reason interfaces exist to my mind and attempting to replace them with abstract classes instead could lead to hampered interoperability. Users of any library will thank you if you follow this pattern, even though it may feel like you are repeating yourself at the time.

This is the first time we are using `__invoke()` to control how `fmap()` applies a function to the wrapped value. In the case of `Just`, it simply calls the supplied function against the wrapped value and returns a new instance of `Just` containing the result. To support this style, we must also make a few more changes to our `fmap()` function:

```php
class NotAFunctorException extends Exception {}
function fmap($function, $functor) {
    if(!$functor instanceOf FunctorInterface) {
        throw new NotAFunctorException(
            'fmap must be passed a Functor'
        );
    }
    return $functor($function);
}
```

To stop illegal usage of this function, it will throw an exception if the value passed to it does not implement the `FunctorInterface` we created previously. It then simply calls the functor and passes in the function to be applied. This is where the `__invoke()` method in the `Just` type class steps in and performs the actual function application against the wrapped value and returns a new instance of `Just` containing the results.

Here is an example that puts our new `fmap()` and `Just` functionality to the test:

```php
fmap($x, new Just(2)); // Just(4);
```

At this point, it makes sense to review the two laws that govern what a functor must do and how it must appear to surrounding code. The first functor law ensures that the `fmap()` function itself does not change the returned value, for only `$x()` in our example is allowed to work on the contained value. This can be written in a formulaic manner as `fmap id = id`, which will make more sense when addressed in the example code further on. You can think of `fmap()` as an impartial facilitator which, while it is incredibly important, should have no effect on the final output.

It is also stated in the second law that composing two functions - and subsequently mapping the resulting function over a functor - should be the same as first mapping one function over the function and then mapping the second one. This can be written as `fmap(f . g) = fmap f . fmap g`, and it is essentially a protection against `fmap()` altering the return value.

Let's test the Just functor against these laws to prove its status as a functor, starting with the first law:

```
$id = function($value) {
    return $value;
};
fmap($id, new Just(2)); // Just(2);
$id(new Just(2)); // Just(2);
```

It is immediately clear that we have achieved a pass against the first law. The second law can also be proven for Just:

```
$a = function($value) {
    return $value + 1;
};
$b = function($value) {
    return $value + 2;
};
$c = compose($a, $b);
fmap($c, new Just(2)); // Just(5);
fmap($a, fmap($b, new Just(2))); // Just(5);
```

Once again, you can see that the second law holds as well, and we can congratulate ourselves on having created our first functor. However, we have used more code to reach the same result - why would that ever be useful?

Below, we define the class Nothing, a friendly data type representation of an empty or null value to prove that we can benefit from our new universal style:

```
class Nothing extends Functor {
    public function __invoke($function) {
        return new Nothing;
    }
}
```

I know that was a bit of a letdown, but wait, there's more! What about if we want to work on those lists mentioned earlier?

```php
class Collection extends Functor {
    public function __invoke($function) {
        return new Collection(
            array_map(function($value) use ($function) {
                return $function($value);
            }, $this->container)
        );
    }
}
```

Here, the Collection class represents a wrapped list or array, and the __ invoke() defined within knows how to apply a function to each item in the list. Now you can see the power of abstracting out some of the functionality. Here is an example of this:

```php
$list = new Collection(array(
    1,
    2,
    3,
));
$resultList = fmap($x, $list); // Collection(2, 4, 6)
```

You will have noticed a useful function on the Functor abstract class called get(), and we can use that now to extract the actual value back out of the context:

```php
$array = $resultList->get(); // array(2, 4, 6)
```

Functors are an excellent way of applying functions to esoteric data structures. In the case of the PHP examples we defined earlier, all you have to do is lift the structure in question to become a functor. Once the structure is "functor-ized", you can apply structure-agnostic functions to the contained data and the functor will handle pulling the correct value out of the structure.

Applicatives

20

Now that we have mastered the ins and outs of functors, we can move onto a slightly more complex type called an applicative. Whereas functors applied a function to a wrapped value, applicatives apply a wrapped function to a wrapped value. That may sound pretty crazy, but it is much easier than it sounds.

Similar to the functors, we will need to write some code to unpack the wrapped function before we can apply it to the value. There is, of course, no special PHP syntax to handle this, so we will need some boilerplate handling code to have the same effect. Once again, let us begin by implementing an interface for applicatives:

```php
interface ApplicativeInterface {
    /**
     * Defines how amap() should deal with this data type
     * @param callable $function
     */
    public function __invoke();
}
```

Also, we need the beginnings of our `Applicative` type class, which is essentially a nice simple container for the function we wish to wrap up:

```php
class Applicative implements ApplicativeInterface {
    protected $function;
    public function __construct($function) {
        $this->set($function);
    }
    public function set($function) {
        $this->function = $function;
    }
    public function get() {
        return $this->function;
    }
}
```

Now we need to tell the applicative equivalent of `fmap()`, called `amap()`, to apply its wrapped function to the supplied values by adding an __invoke() method to Applicative. You might have missed that, unlike functors, applicatives can handle functions that expect multiple parameters!

```php
public function __invoke() {
    if(func_get_arg(0) instanceOf ApplicativeInterface) {
        $function = $this->get();
        foreach(func_get_args() as $arg) {
            if($arg instanceOf ApplicativeInterface) {
                $function = compose($function, $arg->get());
            }
        }
        return new static($function);
    } else {
        return call_user_func_array($this->get(),
            func_get_args());
    }
}
```

So here you can see the contortions that are required to support composition of applicatives and multiple parameters in PHP, but take a moment to read through it, and it should start to make sense.

The first case that __invoke() handles is the composition of Applicative instances into one super Applicative. In the second case, we are applying the function that was wrapped in Applicative ($this-> function in the example) to an array of supplied parameters.

The next step is to define the amap() function itself so that we can begin actually using the Applicative type class:

```php
class NotAnApplicativeException extends Exception {}
function amap($applicative) {
    $func_name = __FUNCTION__;
    $params = array_slice(func_get_args(), 1);
    if(is_array($applicative)) {
        return array_map(function($actual_applicative)
            use ($func_name, $params) {
                array_unshift($params, $actual_applicative);
                return call_user_func_array($func_name, $params);
            }, $applicative);
    }
    if($applicative instanceOf ApplicativeInterface) {
        return call_user_func_array($applicative, $params);
    } else {
        throw new NotAnApplicativeException($func_name
            . ' must be called with an applicative');
    }
}
```

It is far more complicated than `fmap()`, as you might expect, so I will work through it step-by-step to describe what is happening.

First, it gets its own function name and stores it into a variable for later use. It is also grabbing all the parameters passed to the function except for the first one. Here comes some more good news, `amap()` can apply more than one `Applicative` to the parameters!

All you have to do is pass in an array of `Applicatives` as the first parameter to `amap()`, and it will handle the rest. This is why you can see it iterating over an array using `array_map()` before indirectly calling itself.

Next up is the code to handle the actual call against the `Applicative` `__invoke()` method, which is sitting inside a check against the `ApplicativeInterface` to ensure the correct type is being passed in.

As you can see, all the parameters for the `amap()` function are passed into the `Applicative` to be applied against the contained function. This means that if you are passing in three parameters, then the function wrapped in `Applicative` should be able to handle three parameters. If you do not supply the correct number of arguments, then a PHP error will be triggered. Unfortunately, this is where our PHP emulation of applicative functionality is a little flaky.

Now let us review the applicative laws and attempt to verify our implementations against them. I will only attempt to prove two of the laws here as the other two, seen below, are difficult and complex to emulate in PHP.

```
pure (.) <*> u <*> v <*> w = u <*> (v <*> w)
u <*> pure y = pure ($ y) <*> u
```

Fortunately, we can create enough of an applicative for demonstration purposes and to convey the ideas required here.

The first law is equivalent to that which we saw earlier for functors `pure id` `<*> v = v`, which translates to the following PHP code further clarified in Figure 20.1, Figure 20.2, and Figure 20.3:

```php
$id = function($value) {
    return $value;
};
$v = new Just(2);
```

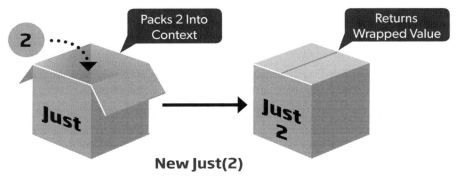

Figure 20.1 : Creating a New `Just` Context

```php
$app_id = new Applicative($id); // pure id
```

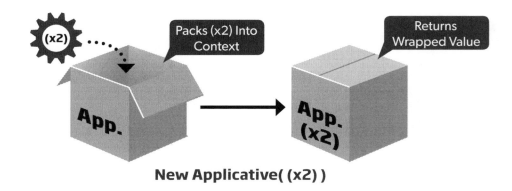

Figure 20.2 : Inserting a Function into an Applicative Context

```
$result = amap($app_id, $v); // <*> v
// $result = Just(2);
// So $result === $v thus proving the law
```

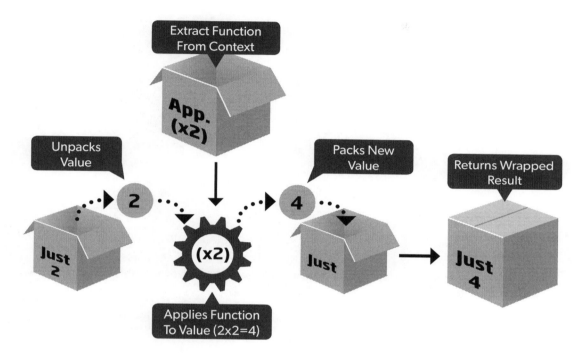

Figure 20.3 : Mapping the applicative

From that result, we can infer that calling the $id()$ function after it has been packed up into an Applicative context against $v will yield $v, and we have therefore proven the first identity law. Much like with the functor example earlier, this ensures that packing a function into a context and applying it using amap() does not affect the returned value. It is the responsibility of the function being applied to change the value.

Next up is a check of homomorphism by checking adherence to pure f <*> pure x = pure (f x), which roughly translates as:

```php
$f = function($value) {
    return $value + 1;
};
$x = function($value) {
    return $value + 2;
};
$pure_f = new Applicative($f); // pure f
$pure_x = new Applicative($x); // pure x
$result = amap($pure_f, $pure_x); // pure f <*> pure x
// $result = Applicative();
$pure_fx = new Applicative(function($value) use ($f, $x) {
    return $f($x($value));
}); // pure (f x)
// $pure_fx = Applicative();
// $pure_fx should === $result
$result(1); // 4
$pure_fx(1); // 4
```

The PHP emulation of Applicative does appear to meet this law from the outside, but it is important to note that the shape of the context differs between them even though the result is the same.

So to wrap up, if you will pardon the pun, applicatives are like functors on steroids - they pack an extra punch! Functors allow you to apply a function to a value wrapped up in a context, but applicatives can also apply a wrapped function to one or more wrapped values.

Monads, Monoids

Extending this idea further, you approach the concept of monads. With an understanding of functors and applicatives, you should be able to pick up on the internal operations of a monad more easily, so if you do not have a good grasp on those concepts yet, then I recommend you review them before continuing here.

Monads can be a difficult concept to approach, and the three associated laws only help to deepen the misunderstanding that surrounds them. To ease the learning curve, I am going to forgo the formalities and focus on the results. This may not be purely functional code, but the idea is to get you on the way to understanding monads.

To begin with, let's address the elephant in the room. The reason most often cited for using a monad is that you can maintain state, but it is just one benefit. They also provide a repeatable way to use functions that, at the outset, are incompatible with each other.

Monads may not necessarily be as useful in PHP when compared to purely functional languages. In PHP, there are other ways of handling the problems that monads address with better support from the language. Just because it does not necessarily directly translate to a real world use case, however, does not mean it should not be explored and learned about using a familiar programming language. It is a hidden secret that any language that has closures and anonymous functions can produce monads!

The intention of covering monads is to, hopefully, build emulations that will help you to understand similar concepts in functional languages should you wish to explore them. Who knows, you might even find them really useful in a PHP project at some point anyway.

With the disclaimer out of the way, let's dig in and review the core principles that define a monad. There are three universal mathematical laws, but we will address those later as they make it harder to grasp the concepts. A monad is a design pattern where a function returns a wrapped value when fed a wrapped value, which sounds just like the functors or applicatives we have already seen, but there is a gimmick or two, of course.

Where a functor or an applicative will return the result of a function application by repackaging it into the same context, there is no such rule to constrain our new friend the monad. It can take a function that returns a different context and wrestle it into submission. Not only will it apply this function but the monadic nature of the construct will assist in chaining up functions to be applied to the wrapped value.

Monads do not actually manipulate any of the values in the container as this is the job of the functions you ask it to apply. Just like an applicative, it just knows how to apply the supplied function, but does not actually know or define any of the filtering logic.

For the purposes of simplicity, we must keep in mind the following guidelines while constructing any monad in PHP. A monad maintains a container - an example of a container that we have already seen is the `Just` functor we defined earlier.

In addition, a monad defines two functions that allow us to manipulate that protected container. The first of which is a function to inject a value into the aforementioned container so that the monad can wrap up a value. In Haskell, this is defined as `return`, but we are going to call it `pack()` as it describes the action more clearly to my mind as we are packing the value into a container.

Finally, when we want to apply a function to the values stored in the container, we are going use a method called `map()`, which is the equivalent of Haskell's `bind()`.

Now you have a basic description of what a monad is and its various constituent parts. All monads define these basics, but of course, each has their own implementation details that may expose various other methods for consumption.

Your First Monad

Confusing? I'll wager that you are still scratching your head, so let's look at some code and check out a monad in action. We are going to redefine the Just functor from earlier as a monad in its own right - to prevent a name collision, we will call it Only as it only contains a simple value.

The container aspect of Only looks like this:

```php
class Only {
    protected $container = null;
    public function __construct($value) {
        $this->container = $value;
    }
    public function get() {
        return $this->container;
    }
}
```

The second step of the monad process is to implement our pack() method, which will accept a new value to insert into a container of Only. Add the following method to the class definition:

```php
public static function pack($value) {
    return new static($value);
}
```

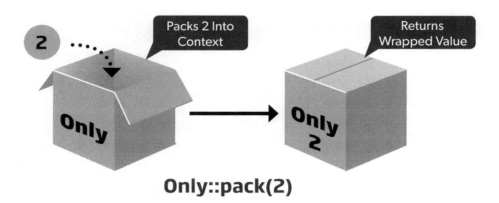

Figure 21.1 : Only::pack() in Action

Next up is the definition of the map() method that you will remember applies a function to the value inside our Only monad:

```php
public function map($function) {
    return $function($this->container);
}
```

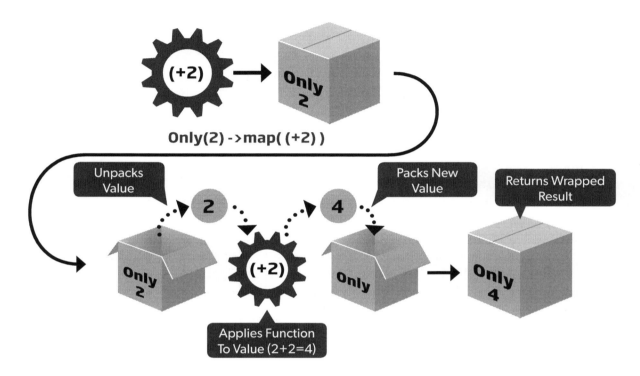

Figure 21.2 : map() Facilitating Function Application

Functions passed to the map() method of Only are given access to the container's contents, and it is important that they not be allowed to leak any values beyond these walls. This means that the monad must wrap up the result of the function in a monad.

Believe it or not, you have defined your first, admittedly very simple, monad! Remember those pesky laws I mentioned? Let's verify our Only monad against them.

The Three Monadic Laws

Firstly, executing map( ) on a freshly wrapped value (pack( )) must yield the same result as giving the value directly to the function you are applying. To make this a little clearer, imagine we have two functions $x( ) and $y( ) that accept a value, process it, and pass back a wrapped computation. Keeping the first law in mind, pack( ) is a left identity for map( ), which can be programmatically defined as:

```
Only::pack(2)->map($x);
```

This must have the same result as directly applying the function to the same value unwrapped:

```
$x(2);
```

Secondly, passing in a function that does not operate on the supplied value, but only applies pack( ) to it must return precisely the same values bound up in a monad. This means that pack( ) is a right identity for map( ):

```
$only = Only::pack(2);
$only_applied = $only->map(function($value) {
    return Only::pack($value);
});
// $only === $only_applied
```

This is a basic protection against pack( ) or map( ) affecting the value as nothing should change the result except for the anonymous filtering function itself.

Thirdly, nesting map( ) calls must produce the same result as when they are called sequentially. To put this another way, if you chain calls to map( ), you should get the same result as calling them in a nested function. This can be illustrated with PHP code like so:

```
$only = Only::pack(2)->map($x)->map($y);
```

Which must be functionally equivalent to:

```
$only = Only::pack(2)->map(function($value) use ($x, $y) {
    return $x($value)->map(function($value) use ($y) {
        return $y($value);
    });
});
```

Hopefully, you have endured the pseudocode unscathed and have come out the other side understanding the basics of the three laws for creating a bona fide monad. Now all that remains is to test our Only monad against these laws to verify its status as a genuine monad.

To prove the first law, the variables $a and $b in the following code must contain the same result:

```
$x = function($value) {
    return $value + 2;
};
$a = Only::pack(2)->map($x); // 4
$b = $x(2); // 4
```

As you can see, they both contain the same result: an integer of 4. That proves law one!

On to law two, we must prove that a function returns an instance of Only:

```
$a = Only::pack(2); // Only(2)
$b = $a->map(function($value) {
    return Only::pack($value);
}); // Only(2)
```

In this case, both $a and $b should contain the same wrapped value in the same shaped context. In the case of Only, we have proven that they definitely do.

So now, we get to the third and final law that our monad must adhere to - being called sequentially is the same as being called in a nested manner:

```
$only = Only::pack(2);
$a = $only->map($x)->map($y); // Only(20)
$b = $only->map(function($value) use ($x, $y) {
    return $x($value)->map(function($value) use ($y) {
        return $y($value);
    });
}); // Only(20)
```

Thankfully, our Only monad has also proven itself a match for the third law, and we have successfully proven that you have written your first monad. Congratulations!

Maybe We Can Have a Second Monad

With the basics down pat, it is time to move onto something more challenging and useful. As you have already seen the php-option library in *Handling Your NULLs*, we will introduce a monad-style solution to the same concepts.

However, firstly, let's briefly review the issue we are trying to solve. When coding, it is common to make requests to external resources - such as databases or files - which may or may not return a result:

```
$sth = $pdo->prepare("SELECT * FROM umuntu");
$sth->execute();
$row = $sth->fetch(PDO::FETCH_LAZY);
echo 'Name: ';
if($row) {
   echo $row->ibizo . ' (verified)';
} else {
   echo 'Unknown';
}
```

The example code illustrates a simple database query to fetch a person's first name from the person table. If there is no result, then it simply prints out "Name: Unknown", but if a name is found, then it should append the label "(verified)" to the person's name, rendering "Name: Marion (verified)".

It becomes very tiresome to always check the return values of each call to a resource that may or may not exist, and it is much easier to always assume that it does. In Haskell, this is known as the Maybe monad, and we will simulate it here in PHP.

Once again, the Maybe monad is essentially a simple container much like the Only monad we defined earlier.

```
class Maybe {
   protected $container = null;
   public function __construct($value) {
      $this->set($value);
   }
   public function get() {
      return $this->container;
   }
   public function set($value) {
      $this->container = $value;
   }
}
```

To this, we will add a couple of custom methods to form the basis of a Maybe construct, but firstly, let's define our pack() and map() methods for this particular monad.

```
public static function pack($value) {
    return new static($value);
}
public function map($function) {
    return $this->isNothing() ?
        $this :
        static::pack($function($this->container));
}
```

As the pack() method is exactly the same as the one we already created for Only, let's just skip over that and concentrate on the minor customizations to map(). If the result is nothing (isNothing() will be defined shortly), then the monad simply returns itself without applying the supplied function. Should there be a genuine value in the container, the function will be applied and the new value will be returned wrapped up in a Maybe context.

```
public function isNothing() {
    return (null === $this->container);
}
```

The isNothing() method simply checks if the contained value is null and returns a Boolean.

```
public function getOrElse($default) {
    return $this->isNothing() ?
        $default :
        $this->container;
}
```

Maybe gets more interesting once you define the getOrElse() method as it allows you to return a default value if the container is empty or the contained value if there is one. To illustrate this functionality in action, here is the imperative example implemented using the Maybe monad instead of an imperative if else:

```
$sth = $pdo->prepare("SELECT * FROM umuntu");
$sth->execute();
$row = $sth->fetch(PDO::FETCH_LAZY);
$verify_names = function($value) {
    return $value->ibizo . ' (verified)';
};
echo 'Name: ' . Maybe::pack($row)->
    map($verify_names)->
    getOrElse('Unknown');
```

Just as in the imperative example, when there is no row available, this code will echo "Name: Unknown". If there is a record, it will display "Name: Marion (verified)". The advantage of using the monad in this case is that it could be chained with other function applications, the code to add the verified label can be easily reused elsewhere, and the code is arguably easier to read and simpler to write.

Writer Monad

When working with pure PHP functions, it can be useful to add some debugging information to them for logging purposes. As we are inside a pure function, we must not attempt to set state or cause any side effects such as printing directly to screen. All of our functions should pass their output as return values. You need a construct to add flexibility to your functions - the Writer monad.

The Writer monad allows you to write out to screen, disk, memory, etc. whilst also maintaining the method chain and common interface. To show this in action, we will need at least two simple functions that we can apply to the Writer monad.

Our first function is a simple method, stripping non-alpha characters from a string:

```
$strip = function($x) {
    return preg_replace('/[^a-z]/i', '', $x);
};
```

Let's apply this function to an actual value so we can see it in action:

```
$str = 'Akl;^(&^EW(&W)Ehdbnjd33445454nbgfwoqf';
echo $strip($str); // AklEWWEhdbnjdnbgfwoqf
```

To compliment this functionality, the second function will convert the supplied string to base 64:

```
$str = 'AklEWWEhdbnjdnbgfwoqf';
$base64 = function($x) {
    return base64_encode($x);
};
echo $base64($str); // QWtsRVdXRWhkYm5qZG5iZ2Z3b3Fm
```

Both of these functions take the same number of arguments and return the same value type, which makes them composable functions without further modification. The return value of one function can be passed directly into the other as an argument. To demonstrate this ability, we must use the compose() function we defined earlier:

```
$strip_base64 = compose($strip, $base64);
echo $strip_base64($str); // QWtsRVdXRWhkYm5qZG5iZ2Z3b3Fm
```

As you can see, the return value is as expected - the same as if you had called echo $base64($strip($str)). Suppose for a moment we did not know that, and we were curious to know which function was being applied to $str first. To prove our hypothesis, we can use logging to determine the call order of the functions.

The first thing you would normally do in PHP is to add statements printing out a message to screen from each function, but as I mentioned before, that is cheating and breaks pure functions! For this example, you are to wipe that knowledge from your mind. We will add logging strings as return values from the functions instead.

```
$strip = function($x) {
    return array(
        preg_replace('/[^a-z]/i', '', $x),
        'Non-alphas stripped from string',
    );
};
$base64 = function($x) {
    return array(
        base64_encode($x),
        'Encoding the string to base64',
    );
};
```

Now that we have logging in place, we can compose the functions again and try the same string manipulations again:

```
$strip_base64 = compose($strip, $base64);
echo $strip_base64($str);
```

Unfortunately, the logging has broken our function composition and triggers a PHP error:

```
PHP Warning:  base64_encode() expects parameter 1 to be
    string, array given
```

Our functions only accept one string parameter, and we are now trying to stuff an array into one of them. This is what you expect PHP to do, but it is not what we want.

Immediately, you are probably thinking of ways to work around this annoyance. At least one method revolves around modifying the second function ($base64) to accept an array as its first parameter, but this would change the function's signature. It would also mean that you would not be able to compose the functions in reverse order.

The next option you are probably thinking about is to write a wrapping function that calls both functions internally and combines the result. It will work, but it is not as flexible as it could be - think again of the possible need to reverse the composition in the future or other methods of reuse.

Instead, let's write a higher order compose function specifically for handling these function signatures. It will accept the two string functions we created earlier as arguments and return a composed function.

```php
$compose_log = function($f, $g) {
    return function($x) use($f, $g) {
        $fx = $f($x);
        $y  = $fx[0]; // AklEWWEhdbnjdnbgfwoqf
        $s  = $fx[1]; // Non-alphas stripped from string
        $gy = $g($y);
        $z  = $gy[0]; // QWtsRVdXRWhkYm5qZG5iZ2Z3b3Fm
        $t  = $gy[1]; // Encoding the string to base64
        return array($z, $s . $t);
    };
};
$strip_base64 = $compose_log($strip, $base64);
$j = $strip_base64($str);
// array(
//     "QWtsRVdXRWhkYm5qZG5iZ2Z3b3Fm",
//     "Non-alphas stripped from stringEncoding the string to
//         base64"
// )
```

This can be improved still further, however, by converting or lifting our functions to interoperable debug functions rather than writing custom composing functions.

Essentially, the function signature of the original function was:

```
f:String = String
```

With our most recent modifications, we have created:

```
f:String = [String, String]
```

However, we want to convert them so that the signature changes to:

```
f:[String, String] = [String, String]
```

In this way, it is possible to use the universal compose() function rather than some custom logic each time to compose individual cases.

This is where we introduce the naming conventions we used in the Only and Maybe monads we have already seen. The first order of business is lifting the value passed into each function so that it is an array. By default, the log is set to an empty string.

```
public static function pack($value, $log = '') {
    return new static(array($value, $log));
}
```

Lifting the functions to accept an array as a parameter and then applying it is the job of the map() method.

```
public function map($f) {
    $x = $this->container[0];
    $s = $this->container[1];
    $fx = $f($x);
    $y = $fx[0];
    $t = $fx[1];
    return static::pack($y, $s . $t);
}
```

Now let's see our latest monad in action by wrapping our string in a new `Writer` monad:

```
$Wstr = Writer::pack($str);
// Writer(
//     array(
//         "Ak1;^(&^EW(&W)Ehdbnjd33445454nbgfwoqf",
//         ""
//     )
// )
```

To use our monad, we need to apply a function to it, so let's start with `$strip()` again:

```
$Wstr2 = $Wstr->map($strip);
// Writer(
//     array(
//         "Ak1EWWEhdbnjdnbgfwoqf",
//         "Non-alphas stripped from string"
//     )
// )
```

Finally for the pièce de résistance, we can chain our call to `$base64()` onto the result from `$strip()`:

```
$Wstr3 = $Wstr2->map($base64);
// Writer(
//     array(
//         "QWtsRVdXRWhkYm5qZG5iZ2Z3b3Fm",
//         "Non-alphas stripped from stringEncoding the string
//             to base64"
//     )
// )
```

As you can clearly see from the results, we now have a `Writer` monad that contains exactly the same values that we achieved via our custom composition function (`$compose_log()`). From here, you have the tools to create new monads for various other pieces of functionality. My suggestion is that the `Reader` and `State` monads are probably the next most useful, so I would recommend starting there.

22

Event-driven Programming

One well-established use of functional-style code is in event-driven programming. If you have written JavaScript code before, you will likely have previous experience with this paradigm.

Functions such as `setInterval()` and `onClick()` are just two such examples that make use of an event-driven approach in JavaScript. This is not a method of working that PHP easily supports out of the box, but thankfully, there a few extensions and libraries out there to help.

The functional approach of removing and avoiding state is a major advantage when dealing with asynchronous code. Of course, it would also be much more difficult to create such programs if simple functional constructs - such as lambdas and closures - were not available to handle callback duties.

In the PECL repository, there are a number of extensions intended to provide PHP with non-blocking I/O functionality such as libevent, eio, event, and ev. In terms of libraries, there is ReactPHP (you might recognize this name from the partial function application section) and a few other less well known options.

For the purposes of demonstration, we will use ReactPHP (http://reactphp.org) here as it is easier to install and does not have any additional server requirements like the aforementioned PECL extensions (which are also worth checking out, though!).

ReactPHP Installation

Installation is incredibly simple with the help of Composer. In a fresh directory, you can run:

```
curl -s http://getcomposer.org/installer | php
php composer.phar init --require=react/http:0.3.* -n
php composer.phar install
```

Composer will install the ReactPHP components for use in your project.

Getting Started

Just like with earlier examples of Composer installed libraries, you need to add the vendor autoloading to your file (`server.php`) first.

```
require 'vendor/autoload.php';
```

Then, we can get on with the business of setting up a simple web server, which - at its heart - is a long running PHP process. When a request is made to the server, this bubbles up as an event and triggers the actioning callback. If you have previous experience with NodeJS, then this pattern will be very familiar to you.

Firstly, we will define a simple request-handling function that just returns a string:

```
$rh = function($request, $response) {
    $response->writeHead(200, array(
        'Content-Type' => 'text/plain'
    ));
    $response->end("Sakubona, unjani?");
};
```

Next up is the actual web server itself and the necessary event loop to turn it into a long-running process:

```
$loop = React\EventLoop\Factory::create();
$socket = new React\Socket\Server($loop);
$http = new React\Http\Server($socket, $loop);
```

Finally, we must bind the request handler (`$rh`) to the server (`$http`), set a socket for the server to listen to, and set the event loop in motion:

```
$http->on('request', $rh);
$socket->listen(7355);
$loop->run();
```

The server can now be started on the command line quite simply with php server.php. You can now access the server on http://127.0.0.1:7355, and you will receive a simple plain-text response of "Sakubona, unjani?".

The library is a high-level abstraction above code that can be written in PHP with the `stream_*()` functions, but if you install `libevent` or `libev`, then it will use their C implementations as faster back ends. The HTTP server we have defined here could be written in the following way with pure PHP code:

```php
$srv = stream_socket_server('tcp://127.0.0.1:7355');
while($sh = stream_socket_accept($srv, -1)) {
    fwrite($sh, "HTTP/1.1 200 OK\r\n\r\n");
    fwrite($sh, "Sakubona, unjani?\n");
    fclose($sh);
}
```

It is important to note that ReactPHP has added a number of logical higher-level abstractions and an event loop into the mix, whereas this pure PHP example is as bare bones as it gets, so they are not completely interchangeable examples.

Add Some Logging

As fantastic as it is to get a response from our HTTP server in a web browser, it would be nice if we could also log each and every request for the purposes of debugging. The trouble is that we have a nice pure function that is used to handle the response to an HTTP request, and we do not want to place another concern (logging) into such a tidy function. We can make use of a closure to combine the calls to our functions.

First up is the logging function, which just writes the request method (GET, POST, etc.) and the request path (/, /page-name) to a log file called access_log:

```php
$lh = function($request) {
    $fh = fopen('access_log', 'a');
    fwrite($fh,
        "{$request->getMethod()}: {$request->getPath()}\n");
    fclose($fh);
};
```

We can also make a minor change to the definition of the request handler ($rh) so that it only takes the one parameter ($response) that it actually needs:

```php
$rh = function($response) {
    $response->writeHead(200, array(
        'Content-Type' => 'text/plain'
    ));
    $response->end("Sakubona, unjani?");
};
```

To map the functions, we will wrap them up in a handy closure so that they can be called subsequently to each other:

```
$eh = function($request, $response) use($rh, $lh) {
    $rh($response);
    $lh($request);
};
```

Finally, update the request handler binding line to:

```
$http->on('request', $eh);
```

If you now execute this code by visiting http://127.0.0.1:7355 in your browser, you will be presented with the same message, but your log file will contain something like:

```
GET: /
GET: /favicon.ico
```

The second request is just the web browser being hopeful and trying to find a favicon on our server. Of course, there is not one on our server, but without logging, we would never have known that the server was being hit twice on each request.

Introduce a Monad

So far, we have set up a simple web server with a small amount of functional code. Next up, we have an urgent demand for our server to process user requests. Now of course, the following code is not really written with production in mind and serves more as a jumping off point and example of monad usage.

Since you have already seen the `Maybe` monad, we will take that idea and extend it a little bit by combining it with a list monad. This will provide predictable access to the `GET` parameters that are passed in the request to our little ReactPHP web server. For transparency's sake, this monad will be named `QueryList`. As you may predict, it will be a container for the query string array.

Like the last container monad, we must first define the basic constructor and class property to act as our container.

```php
class QueryList {
    protected $container = null;
    public function __construct(array $value) {
        $this->container = $value;
    }
}
```

In this case, the pack() function is very simple as it just accepts an array and returns the same array wrapped up in a new QueryList container.

```php
public static function pack($value) {
    return new static($value);
}
```

Again, the map() method is really quite simple in the case of this monad. It takes the contained array and simply uses array_map() to apply a function to each value in the array before returning them in a QueryList context.

```php
public function map($f) {
    return static::pack(array_map($f, $this->container));
}
```

With the basic monad functions out of the way, it is time to put problem-specific methods in place. The first of these is the isNothing() method, which we saw in the Maybe monad.

For our QueryList monad, we must make a couple of modifications to facilitate the checks that are required. The code must know if the whole container is empty or - if supplied - if a particular index in the container is nothing.

```php
public function isNothing($index = null) {
    return (null === $index) ?
        !(count($this->container)) :
        !(array_key_exists($index, $this->container));
}
```

As you can see, this is done through the use of a ternary to determine if an index has been supplied and a simple, in-place Boolean checks against the existence in/of the container. This method, much like in the Maybe example, will be used later internally, but it can also be useful publicly as well.

To be able to obtain a value from the container, we must add a get method, much like in the Maybe monad. There is, of course, one very slight change to handle obtaining a particular index from the contained array if the optional $index parameter is supplied.

```
public function get($index = null) {
   return (null === $index) ?
      $this->container :
      $this->container[$index];
}
```

To make our access more robust, we will also create a simple little getOrElse() method, which will give us access to an index or the whole array. If the requested aspect of the container isNothing(), then it will return the supplied default value instead. Again, this is, of course, a very similar method to the similarly-named function in the Maybe monad.

```
public function getOrElse($index = null,
   $default = array()) {
   return ($this->isNothing($index)) ?
      $default :
      $this->get($index);
}
```

There you have it - a custom monad written for the job at hand. As you know, it is built upon the groundwork in the Maybe monad and has been slightly augmented with list-processing specific functionality.

This allows us to easily wrap up the GET query items in a robust container to facilitate easy universal access. Not only that - it also provides a very handy way of applying functions to the internal list. To that end, let us now define a simple lambda to wrap htmlspecialchars().

```
$html_escape = function($string) {
   $flags = ENT_COMPAT;
   if(version_compare(PHP_VERSION, '5.4.0', '>=')) {
      $flags |= ENT_HTML5;
   }
   return htmlspecialchars($string, $flags, 'UTF-8');
};
```

In order to support UTF-8 in PHP 5.3 and still set the correct document type flag for PHP 5.4, we must have some simple version checking logic. This means that we have ended up with a very basic wrapping function that we can now apply/map against our QueryList monad.

Before we can do that, however, we must define the ReactPHP server that will supply its GET parameters to us. Just like last time, we need to implement an event handler:

```
$eh = function($request, $response) use ($html_escape) {
    $ql = QueryList::pack($request->getQuery());
    $ql = $ql->map($html_escape);
    $response->writeHead(200, array(
        'Content-Type' => 'text/html'
    ));
    $response->end($ql->getOrElse('foo', 'A default value'));
};
```

At the moment, this simply takes in the request, extracts the query parameters, and packs them into a QueryList monad. We then map $html_escape() to each value in the array, which goes through applying htmlspecialchars(). The code then plucks one particular index and prints that as the response.

Of course, none of this will run until we set up ReactPHP's event loop and bind the event handler $eh():

```
$loop = React\EventLoop\Factory::create();
$socket = new React\Socket\Server($loop);
$http = new React\Http\Server($socket, $loop);
$http->on('request', $eh);
$socket->listen(7355);
$loop->run();
```

With that complete you can start the server on the command line as before and visit http://127.0.0.1:7355?foo=bar to see bar printed to your web page. To see the $html_escape() lambda in action, we will need to pass in some URL-encoded special characters instead of bar:

```
http://127.0.0.1:7355?foo=%3Cbang%3E
```

This will print the result (<bang>) to screen in a properly HTML-encoded manner.

Now you have seen some event-driven programming and employed a monad to save yourself from painful list interactions, but what is that hiding around the corner? Callback hell! If you have ever written in an event-driven way before, you have probably encountered the issue of having deeply-nested callback functions rendering illegible code. There are a few patterns we can use to avoid this issue that will be covered in the next section.

Callback Wrangling

Event-driven programming, if left to its own devices, can quickly enter a stage known as callback hell. Unfortunately, the next level is certain death… or a major refactor, as the following highly-contrived code exemplifies:

```
function a($v, $cb) { return $cb($v) . 'a'; }
function b($v, $cb) { return $cb($v) . 'b'; }
function c($v, $cb) { return $cb($v) . 'c'; }
function d($v, $cb) { return $cb($v) . 'd'; }
$res = a('ndlovu', function($v) {
    return b(ucwords($v), function($v) {
        return c(strrev($v), function($v) {
            return d(str_repeat($v, 3), function($v) {
                return $v;
            });
        });
    });
});
echo $res; // uvoldNuvoldNuvoldNdcba
```

You can save yourself from this right from the start by adopting some predefined patterns in the code you are producing. To make this deal sweeter, there are some simple, but powerful libraries that make it easier to implement these patterns. This allows you to concentrate on your code, abstracting the problem away.

We are going to review two such libraries that have two different approaches to the problem. They are both part of the greater ReactPHP project although they are emulations of two different JavaScript libraries.

Async

Starting with the simpler of the two libraries, Async, which is a PHP implementation of the ideas in async.js. It simplifies callbacks by allowing you to define them as lists rather than being nested within each other. Much as before, installation is relatively simple when using Composer in the same directory you experimented with the ReactPHP web server earlier:

```
php composer.phar require react/async:~1.0
```

You can either call the functions in parallel or as a waterfall. By using the parallel implementation, you are effectively passing the same call to a set of functions and combining their results in the order they are returned, rather than the order they are defined. This is demonstrated clearly in this example from the project's documentation:

```php
use React\Async\Util as Async;
$loop = React\EventLoop\Factory::create();
Async::parallel(
    array(
        function ($callback, $errback) use ($loop) {
            $loop->addTimer(1, function () use ($callback) {
                $callback('Slept for a whole second');
            });
        },
        function ($callback, $errback) use ($loop) {
            $loop->addTimer(1, function () use ($callback) {
                $callback('Slept for another whole second');
            });
        },
        function ($callback, $errback) use ($loop) {
            $loop->addTimer(1, function () use ($callback) {
                $callback('Slept for yet another whole second');
            });
        },
    ),
    function (array $results) {
        foreach ($results as $result) {
            var_dump($result);
        }
    },
    function (\Exception $e) {
        throw $e;
    }
);
$loop->run();
// string(24) "Slept for a whole second"
// string(34) "Slept for yet another whole second"
// string(30) "Slept for another whole second"
```

The waterfall model is different because it will pass the return value from the preceding function as a parameter into the next one. In this way, the functions return their results in the order they were defined. The following example is again taken from the documentation of the React/Async project:

```php
use React\Async\Util as Async;
$loop = React\EventLoop\Factory::create();
$addOne = function ($prev, $callback = null) use ($loop) {
    if (!$callback) {
        $callback = $prev;
        $prev = 0;
    }
    $loop->addTimer(1, function () use ($prev, $callback) {
        $callback($prev + 1);
    });
};
Async::waterfall(array(
    $addOne,
    $addOne,
    $addOne,
    function ($prev, $callback) use ($loop) {
        echo "Final result is $prev\n";
        $callback();
    },
));
$loop->run();
// Final result is 3
```

Here you have two simple methods for reigning in wild callback functions, but I promised more! The next library is an implementation of a subset of the functionality found in CommonJS.

Promises

This pattern is known as a promise, and it is a little more complex, but of course, more powerful to boot. A piece of code can make a promise to return a certain value once its asynchronous operation (known as a deferred) is complete. We do not want to delay execution, so we take it at its word and accept a placeholder instead.

This placeholder or promise can be passed from function to function until the result is required to continue execution. In the case of a database write, you can stick it into an asynchronous operation and watch for a result to display a notification or attempt a retry of the save.

React/Promise also makes it possible to manage the processing of many operations. We will only address a small subset of its functionality here, although there is more documentation on the GitHub page for the project (https://github.com/reactphp/promise). The contrived example that follows would actually be broken out through the layers of your application so it is more for illustrative purposes.

Firstly, we need to install React/Promise using Composer, and the installation instructions remain the same as specified previously.

```
php composer.phar require react/promise:~1.0
```

To begin with, we will create a simple logging function called elog( ), which is short for echo log. It will simply take a title, a body, and an option to print or return the formatted log.

```php
function elog($title, $body = '', $return = false) {
    $body = (empty($body)) ?: ": $body\n";
    $log = "\n{$title}{$body}";
    if($return) {
        return $log;
    }
    echo $log;
}
```

Next up is a simple PHP function object that will handle reading a stream from the Unix random source at /dev/urandom. For the sake of being obvious, we will call this class ReadStream:

```php
class ReadStream {
    protected $resolver = null;
    protected $data = null;
}
```

/dev/urandom is a non-blocking source of random binary information on POSIX systems. It is similar in nature to /dev/random, but it is cryptographically less secure as it reuses the internal entropy pool to generate pseudo-random bits. This reuse makes it potentially less secure, but for our purposes, it will do nicely.

If you are following along on a Windows machine, then there is no simple equivalent of /dev/random - or for that matter, /dev/urandom - so you can simply use a large text file as your source for the following examples.

You have a simple class with two properties for later use, so let's add a static method to bind a resolver (a tracking component of the promise library) and return a new instance of ReadStream.

```php
public static function bind($resolver) {
    $that = new static;
    $that->setResolver($resolver);
    return $that;
}
```

The resolver is set using a class method as you saw in the previous code block, so let's define it:

```php
public function setResolver($resolver) {
    $this->resolver = $resolver;
}
```

The final method that is to be added to the ReadStream function object is the magic __invoke() function.

```php
public function __invoke($stream, $loop) {
    $rand = base64_encode(fread($stream, 16));
    $this->data .= $rand;
    $this->resolver->progress($rand);
    if(strlen($this->data) > 1000) {
        $this->resolver->resolve($this->data);
    }
}
```

To break down its operation, we will begin with the first line of the function. It reads 16 bytes from the file stream and then encodes them using base 64. This gives us a string representation of the binary data that is read from the random source.

This is then added to the data class property so that we can maintain some state between asynchronous calls to this function object. As each line of random is processed, the code calls progress() on the promise to log the status of the asynchronous code. Finally, if we have more than one thousand characters of random information, we mark the promise as fulfilled.

To get the random stream first, we must get a file resource handle and set it as a non-blocking stream.

```php
$fh = fopen('/dev/urandom', 'rb');
stream_set_blocking($fh, 0);
```

So far, the code has barely even touched upon the functionality that React/Promise makes available, but this is about to change! It all begins with the declaration of a new deferred promise and a set of callbacks to handle results from the promise's resolver.

```
$deferred = new React\Promise\Deferred;
$deferred->promise()->then(
    function ($result) { return $result; }, // 1
    function ($reason) { elog('Rejected', $reason); }, // 2
    function ($update) { elog('Update', $update); } // 3
)->then(
    function($str) { return elog('Random', $str, true); }
)->then(
    function($str) {  echo $str; }
);
```

The then( ) methods are called in sequence when the promise relays an event such as its progress being updated or it finally being resolved. Let's focus on the latter for now as we see that the result returned from the first then( ) block is passed as the input to the second.

Looking at the first then( ) block, you can see that it accepts three callback functions. The first is called when the promise is successfully resolved. When a promise fails to be resolved, the second function will be called. Progress updates will trigger the third and final callback function.

Returning a value from any of these functions will cause it to be supplied as the input parameter to the respective function in the next then( ) block.

As you can see in the subsequent then( ) block, the callbacks are optional. The second and third then( ) blocks are defined with only the successful callbacks supplied. The workings of these callback functions are so simplistic that I am not going to go into any further detail.

To put this into action, we will need a simple event loop, and as before, React/event-loop fills this need admirably.

```
$loop = React\EventLoop\Factory::create();
$loop->addReadStream($fh, ReadStream::bind($deferred->resolver()));
$loop->run();
```

This creates a new event loop, adds a read stream to it by binding the promise to the file handle, and finally, the loop is run. When executed, the code we have laid out will print a list of updates (in real time) followed by a printout of all the results combined into one long result string.

This is a nice introduction to promises, but it would be remiss of me to skip over the more powerful combinatory functionality React/Promise also provides. To allow me to cover the reduce operation, we will need to define another deferred promise before the event loop.

Firstly, though, we must open a new file resource handle and set it to be a non-blocking stream.

```
$fh2 = fopen('/dev/urandom', 'rb');
stream_set_blocking($fh2, 0);
```

The second deferred is essentially the same as the first, but with references changed to include '2nd'.

```
$second_deferred = new React\Promise\Deferred;
$second_deferred->promise()->then(
    function ($result) { return $result; },
    function ($reason) { elog('2nd Rejected', $reason); },
    function ($update) { elog('2nd Update', $update); }
)->then(
    function($str) { return elog('2nd Random', $str, true); }
)->then(
    function($str) { echo $str; }
);
```

To combine the two promises, we will use a reduce operation by implementing When::reduce(), which takes an array of the deferred as its first parameter. The second parameter is a callback function that performs the combination logic and returns a new deferred promise wrapping the result.

You can then apply then() function blocks to this deferred to gain access to the final result.

```
React\Promise\When::reduce(
    array($deferred, $second_deferred),
    function($ignored, $value) {
        static $temp = '';
        return $temp = $temp . $value;
    }
)->then(
    function($result) {
        elog('Final', $result);
        return $result;
    }
)->then(
    function($result) { elog('Final MD5', md5($result)); }
);
```

The first `then()` block simply `elog()`'s the result of the combination and also returns the result for use in the next `then()` block. The final `then()` block prints out an MD5 hash of the result from the reduce operation.

To execute this code, you will need to bind it to the deferred in the event loop again, like so:

```
$loop = React\EventLoop\Factory::create();
$loop->addReadStream($fh, ReadStream::bind($deferred->resolver()));
$loop->addReadStream($fh2, ReadStream::bind($second_deferred->resolver()));
$loop->run();
```

When this code is run, you will get a debug log for each read from both the first and second `deferred`. Each deferred will then print its result.

Finally, the `When::reduce()` will print a combination of both the first and second deferred along with an MD5 hash of that result. There are a number of other operations you can perform on lists of deferred promises, and these include: `map()`, `some()`, `any()`, `all()`, and more. Each allow you to make different decisions based upon the results from your deferred promise.

Although interesting, it is beyond our scope here to go into further detail, but you can easily use the `reduce()` example as a base to explore the rest of the features of this library. For more information, please see the project's documentation on GitHub (https://github.com/reactphp/promise).

Promises are a very handy way to organize callback functions and prevent them from getting out of control. There are some handy pieces of code to make it easier to handle asynchronous operations in PHP code.

PHP is not known for being event-driven, or for asynchronous operations at all for that matter. Most standard library calls do not run this way - leaving the parser to process the job until it is finished in series. With the help of some libraries, it is possible to bring this power to PHP in an elegant way.

Promises provide one way of helping to mitigate the callback hell that event-driven programming can bring with it.

Wrap Up the Show

Event-driven programming is not only possible in PHP, but thanks to the reactor pattern and ReactPHP, it is easy. Whilst event-driven programming can lead to callback hell, as we have seen, there are a number libraries and patterns you can adopt to avoid this.

Much like functional programming, a lot of the event-driven programming we have reviewed here is experimental. It is fun to play with, but rarely finds itself in production.

There are at least two far more popular alternatives in Node.js (ReactPHP was formerly known as NodePHP) and Python's Twisted. Both of these have seen far more time in production than PHP's event libraries.

This can be attributed to PHP's focus on short-running processes for a web server. Sure, it can be run as a daemon with libraries like PHPDaemon (http://daemon.io) and PHP Simple Daemon (http://github.com/shaneharter/PHP-Daemon), but the supporting tooling, however, is not as mature as the competition.

All of this combines to make it a really small niche in PHP programming, but as Igor Wiedler (ReactPHP's creator) says: anything they can have, we can steal!

Hazards of a Functional Approach in PHP

23

PHP is not a functional language, and therefore, it is more than a lack of syntactic sugar that we must overcome. Or more likely in PHP's case, work around and make do!

As a language, PHP has not evolved to support the use of functions, and there has been a deliberate choice to concentrate development resources on improving the language's object-oriented capabilities. I am not criticizing this; given limited resources, it is important that you focus on aspects that will have the greatest impact. Catering to a minority of PHP developers whilst ignoring the masses would hamper continued uptake of the language and disenfranchise current users.

Having said all this, though, it is, of course, frustrating when a language you are using is not able to cater to the code you wish to implement with it. "Use a more appropriate language!" - you might quite rightly cry.

I would counter that there are a great number of developers who are immensely productive in PHP and may wish to use those skills in a functional style. More practically, there are those of us who must use PHP for various reasons such as it is the only deployment platform, integration with a legacy codebase, or it is an employer's mandate.

All of this means that you will need to think about how you are going to manage your functional projects in PHP. Firstly, how will you layout your files and create functional "packages" for code sharing?

Unfortunately, PHP does not have a mechanism for autoloading functions at present and from following the discussions surrounding two related PHP RFCs, https://wiki.php.net/rfc/autofunc and https://wiki.php.net/rfc/function_autoloading, it would appear the feature is never coming or, at least, is a very long way off.

So that leaves you with a few choices:

- Require/include in all the files for all requests.

- Set up the functions as static methods in a class file, which can then be autoloaded similar to Underscore.php (http://brianhaveri.github.com/Underscore.php/).

- Use my simple functions which cause namespace "use" statements to perform more like an import clause. Whilst it solves a problem, it is - at its core - a complete hack that will invariably slow down your code due to the use of the PHP Tokenizer to double parse the files (https://github.com/treffynnon/namespace-importer).

This is not a show stopper, but it is annoying and does merit mentioning. If you are going to be implementing some basic functional styles, then it does not matter so much, but if you want to share or reuse a whole library of functions, then you are faced with these three horrible options.

Additional caveats include that you cannot simply import one function from a namespace or alias that function in your use statement. You could potentially work around the former by putting each function into its own namespace. You could then simply use that narrower namespace to pull in just the one function.

There is a miserable trade-off, though, as it will make calling the function a more verbose procedure. If you import the parent namespace, for instance, you would need to specify the child namespace before each function call:

```
use Treffynnon as T;
T\Sort\sort($collection, $callable_function);
```

However, it would allow you to pull in just one function like so:

```
use Treffynnon\Sort as TS;
TS\sort($collection, $callable_function);
```

Handling immutable data is complicated by the fact that PHP does not support it natively, and it is the functional developer's responsibility to ensure that they do not introduce state changes into the code themselves. There have been a few attempts to enforce immutable data in PHP, but none of them are particularly satisfactory and all of them require class-based trickery such as Mikko Koppanen's php-immutable extension (https://github.com/mkoppanen/php-immutable) - a self-described hack.

You are now in the uncharted wilds of PHP and pushing the boundaries of what is possible all the time. Things will be sub-optimal at times or just down right impossible, so you will need to use your judgment as to when these techniques are best employed - if at all - in your projects.

Another minor issue is that other PHP developers may struggle to understand your code and curse your name!

Conclusion

This book has introduced you to some functional programming techniques that you can use in your PHP projects today. Whilst this serves as a good primer in a language you know, I would suggest that if you wish to take things further, you should begin looking at other languages such as Haskell, Scala, or Clojure. I find it easier to learn new concepts in a language I am very familiar with, so this has been directed at similar individuals.

In my own projects, I do use some functional methodologies, but those that I have released with open source licenses have so far all been written in object-oriented PHP. This reflects the PHP preference for imperative code over functional programming.

It is also true of my commercial code, although I hope that in the future, these techniques will become more widely understood. We need more functional efforts to be released as open source, more discussions to be had, more speakers to present, and of course, more blog and magazine articles to be written.

That is not to say that there are not any open source projects out there making use of functional constructs in their code. A few examples that I am aware of are ReactPHP (event-driven framework), Bullet (self-described functional web framework), Slim (micro-framework), and Pimple (dependency injection container) - although none of them (to my knowledge) make use of the more complex functional techniques and generally will include the odd lambda or closure here and there. I am sure there are many other projects also using similar code - if you know of an interesting one I have missed, let me know.

If you wish to get involved in the development of functional programming in PHP, the best places to start are the main PHP internals mailing list and the RFCs (https://wiki.php.net/rfc) on the PHP Wiki (https://wiki.php.net). Also functional-php, Underscore.php, and Functionals are all accepting quality pull requests through GitHub.

Resources

- functional-php - https://github.com/lstrojny/functional-php
- React\Curry - https://github.com/reactphp/curry
- nicmart/Functionals - https://github.com/nicmart/Functionals

For functional PHP extras and updates, please check out http://www.functionalphp.com and follow @FunctionalPHP on Twitter.

14660689R00069

Made in the USA
San Bernardino, CA
02 September 2014